KERALA-FOOLS' OWN COUNTRY

RANJITH A M

To my Great fool headed colleagues who speak the wonderful language

Malayaalam

Contents

Contents

Preface

Can I call myself a country within a country

Acknowledgements

I have to acknowledge every person that I have met in my state and every malayalee I have met or have read about. Had it not been for the generosity of most of them, for being accredited fools from generations behind, till date and further, this book could not have been written. I owe myself to those around me who inspire me time and again by happily jumping into the bandwagon of incorrigible fools. I know that their acts of quixotism will never end, and can be the source of literature for generations to come.

My greatest reverence to all those people.

Prologue

Legend says that Kerala was created by Parasurama, the sage, by throwing his mighty axe into the sea. The area up to which his axe went, got converted to land. I have, in this curtain raiser, narrated the innumerable ways by which the most literate, most intelligent, most well-read Keralite is being fooled every day. To add to our cap of fools' feathers, we are inventing on a daily basis, ingenious ways to get ourselves fooled. And the process will go on to a larger extent, when our level of education gets higher and higher up.

You know, pride goes before a fall. And we are very proud, egoistic and most learned.

So we pride ourselves in being more learned fools. We are a fools' own Country.

Jai Parasurama, Jai Kerala

CHAPTER I

Our forefather fools

This is a story which some of you would have heard, either in part or full. Usually this is narrated as a kid's story, but is equally applicable to a lot of us adults too. This part, as an intro, is dedicated to all my fellow Keralites to assess themselves as to which of the characters fit them most. Don't think that you are not one among them. At some situation in your life, you have been more foolish than any of these guys. Read along to remind you of the deeds of your fellow fools.I have rewritten this story for those who have not read it before.

Birbal and the ten foolish men

I am sure most of you know about Emperor Akbar and his very wise minister, Birbal. This is a story attributed to them. Akbar was very proud of himself as a great ruler, and considered his subjects as very intelligent because of his own great wisdom and skillful administration. One day during one of their evening strolls, Akbar opined to Birbal that he was sure that his subjects were very intelligent and there were practically no fools in his country. Birbal objected to this. "No, your Majesty. There are any numbers of fools in this kingdom. " "Okay" said Akbar. "You bring ten great fools from this country to me within seven days, and tell me what act of foolishness they committed. If you cannot find ten of them, let's see" Akbar threatened. They left for the evening to meet again after seven days with details of ten great fools and description of the foolish acts they committed. Birbal set out to fulfill his mission the very next day. He started walking through the streets, meeting all kinds of people. Vendors, workers, rich and poor, and was very happy to see in close quarters, the life of the subjects in his own country. He was all of his own self, without the hassle and tension of being Akbar's minister, attending to the tough situations of the Durbar. Then, he saw a man riding a horse and holding some hay on his own head.

He wondered why he was carrying the load on his head, instead of tying it on the horseback.

'Why do you carry the hay on your head?' Birbal asked.

"Well, you know, I cannot carry it in my hand, because I have to guide the horse by holding on to the reins. But, my horse is very weak and tired. So he cannot carry the weight on his back. So I am carrying it on my head to reduce his load."

Birbal understood the genuineness of the argument and took the name and address of the first fool.

A little later, a man, holding both his hands up, came running and slipped in a muddy spot on the road and fell down flat on his back. He was yelling "Help, help" to other people to help him get up. Birbal noticed that he was not at all hurt, and could easily get up by putting his hands down and lifting himself. But strangely, the man was keeping both hands above his head at the same distance, and will not use them to get up. So then, Birbal went near him. 'Why don't you get up?' asked Birbal.

'I can't,' was the reply.

'Okay, hold on to my hands, and you can get up".

'No, don't do that. Keep my hands free. You can pull me up by lifting me by my hair or any other part of the body."

'Do you have any contagious disease on your hand"? "No, No, No. Hold me up. I will tell you"

Even after getting up, the fellow was holding his hands high above his head. He then explained.

"You see, I have a space in my house, where I want to fix a wooden shelf. The carpenter had asked me to take a measurement of the space and inform him. I measured it and the distance I am holding above my head is the size of the space .So, you can understand that I have to reach the carpenter's house to show him the size of the vacant space. Let me go to his house and show him the size". Birbal took his name and address and allowed him to proceed.

Next day also, he had a similar case of a man running, but this time he was running wildly and hit Birbal and fell down. He was cursing Birbal for obstructing him and spoiling his scientific study.

Birbal was also equally angry and shouted at him. "Why are you running so wild without seeing the road? What is the problem"?

"Any way you have spoilt my study" the man replied. "I will tell you what happened".

“Sir, I was chanting my prayers in the mosque up there, and I wanted to test how far my voice had reached. I was running after my voice, and would have definitely caught it if you had not come in my way. Anyway, I will try once again”.

Birbal had no hesitation and took the man’s name and address. It was the next day morning when birbal spotted the next fool. A man was searching for something in a sandy area beside the road. Birbal asked him what he was searching for. “Well, my friend, I had a golden ring with me. I wanted to save it from thieves when I was away from town. So I dug a hole in this sand and put it in there. Now I have come back and want to take it out. But I am not able to spot it.” “Where did you put it? Do you have a landmark or something else to verify the spot where you dug it in”? Asked Birbal “What do you think? Am I such a fool to dig it in a place without some mark? There was a dark cloud in the shape of a camel just above the place where I put it. But now there is no camel cloud and I cannot spot the location .That’s the problem”. Birbal posed as though he was convinced and took his name and address. That evening, Birbal was coming home after taking an evening stroll. It was already dark and Birbal was in a hurry to reach back. Now, he saw a man searching for something under a street lamp, and stopped to find out what he was searching.

’What have you lost?‘ asked Birbal.

’A ring from my finger.‘ Birbal had in his mind, the previous experience in the morning about a lost ring and so he asked whether he had lost the ring there itself.

’No,‘ ’I dropped it over there, but it’s dark there and there is this light from the street lamp here. So I am searching where there is light”. Birbal got the name of the next fool’s name and address and went home.

Next morning, while still walking, Birbal heard a loud noise. Two men were quarrelling in the middle of the road and were almost coming to blows. Birbal intervened and asked why they were quarreling.

‘Why should this man ask his tiger to attack my buffalo. What did my buffalo do against him or his tiger? I cannot allow this”. So saying ,the man started to attack the second man. Birbal could not see either the buffalo or the tiger. So he asked. “But friends, where is the buffalo and the tiger”. “No, sir, the thing is, we were walking along,’ said the first man, ‘This man asked me what I would choose if God appeared and gave us a wish. You see, I don’t have sufficient wealth, and I am a poor farmer. It would be nice if I have a buffalo. I can take the milk, sell the excess milk, and also use the dung in my farm. So I said that I will get a buffalo from god. Then this man is saying that he will wish for a tiger and let it loose on my buffalo". So saying, they started quarreling again. Now, another thing happened. Amidst them came another man carrying a jar of ghee. The man was watching the conversation and trying to understand the situation. Now he understood what they were fighting for.

'You are a fool to talk to these two fools,' he said to Birbal, and dropped his jar of ghee on the ground. The jar broke, and the ghee ran out.

"If they are not fools" he remarked in bitter anger, "let my bones break like this jar and my blood run out like the ghee" .

Birbal was only happy to collect the names and addresses of all three men.

Birbal took a little rest, and then went to the palace. He asked Akbar to send for the eight men whose names and addresses he had. They all came and Birbal told the stories of them all. Akbar was convinced that all the eight people were genuine fools.

'But there are only eight men here,' said the king. 'I told you to bring ten.'

'All ten are here, your majesty. These are the eight fools. The ninth is I myself. I wasted seven good days in getting these eight fools, so I am also a great fool.'

'But the tenth?' asked Akbar.

'Your majesty, there is one emperor here who ordered me to find ten fools and wasted the time of his minister for seven days. This was the time this birbal should have been using for solving the problems of your majesty's citizens. So, should I say who the tenth fool is?

Akbar laughed aloud and asked

'You mean both of us are fools?'

Yes, your majesty. You, for giving such an order, and me for carrying it out.'

Now, fix up which character fits you most. Ha .. Haa..

CHAPTER II

Kerala is Number one (In blocking Development)

In Kerala, we do not allow any development. Whatever we try, some local thing crops up for the most unexplainable reason. However, we are most experienced in arguing unexplainable things and stick on to it, with a guise of being reasonable. This chapter explains, with the example of a temple reconstruction, how intelligently the reconstruction is blocked perpetually by using a classical paradox.

Kerala has always been lauded for being number one in many things. For example, we are the only state in the country where women outnumber men. We are also great in adult literacy and women literacy. We are good in cleanliness, and also in being one of the few states where many expatriates sweating their life in the desert countries in the gulf and in Europe and America, bring in substantial payments into the banks in Kerala. However, our growth is never in tune with the money and brain power that we have. This is because Keralites are also very good in blocking any developmental programmes. This is also done in ulterior ways, so that it seems that things are done in the most logical way. Everything is hidden in a very wise manner, so that you don't know that you are being stabbed from behind. There is also most illogical, brazen robbery in broad daylight, by raising virtual arguments, which cannot be countered.

I will now tell you just one example. You see, Kerala is probably the only place in the earth, where, getting paid for a hypothetical or virtual job is a right. That is, you don't do anything, somebody else does the job, and you get paid at your doorstep. This you might wonder how. That is called "Nokkukooli", which I will tell you in the next chapter. But beyond that, there is also a wonderful way of blocking development that we Keralites have perfected. The most significant thing about this, is that the poison of stopping developmental works are injected into the system, without the slightest proof that it is against development. What is more, is that the arguments are presented in such a logical fashion that the audience will not know the poison in it, but would be inclined to think that this person has a genuine concern about the topic and that he is putting in a helping hand. But, when the smoke settles down, slowly, the realization would dawn on the end users that the medicine that was prescribed as life saver was actually a killing tablet. The way we deal with things is so characteristic and so innocent looking and innocuous, that it will be impossible to say no to what we propose. It is presented in such a way that it seems very logical and necessary, but invariably, it will lock you up. It applies to industries, factories and all new ventures. You will never understand our logic and its ultimate result. This is because; we are the most literate, most intelligent fools in the world. You must have now become impatient about the verbal cacophony that I have put in till now, but unfortunately, this is how we operate, and you have to live with it . But I will deviate from routine and will tell you one simple story of how as Malayalis (as we call ourselves, based on our language-Malayalam)), we operate to see that nothing is allowed to be done, but at the same time giving a feeling that it was the most logical act to have done this in this very same way.

I will start the story

Once upon a time, there was a temple in a village. It was reasonably famous, and also, with a lot of devotees visiting the shrine. Naturally, there were many people who were involved with the affairs of the temple. As years passed, parts of the temple started deteriorating and needed urgent repairs or renovation. Now, the devotees became concerned about this and they started discussing among themselves on the sorry state of affairs of the temple. So one day, they all assembled in the temple premises to discuss the renovation of the temple. It was generally agreed upon by almost everybody that the current state of the temple is very bad, and the deity may be angered because of the ruining state of the temple. At any cost, the repairs will have to be done immediately to please the deity. It was necessary to entrust the work to a committee to oversee things, collect funds, do the renovation, and to periodically inform the devotees about the progress of work, funds used, remaining fund requirement etc. As is usual, most of the people who supported the renovation , backed out from being members of the committee. However, they offered all possible help to the committee other than being one of the members. This is because the committee members have to visit the houses of the devotees many times and literally beg to each and every one to raise the money for the renovation. Even when the money is there, it is a huge responsibility to supervise the construction. It is easy to criticize by being not in the committee. But somehow, a set of service minded old people were inducted and a committee was formed. Some exceptions were those who volunteered to serve in the committee even without being forced.(You have rightly guessed that these were the members who would, at a later stage, manage the funds, and make some gains out of it.) (We all realise that Gods are in great demand these days and every temple, church, mosque and other religious establishments of all faiths are becoming richer and richer ,and in direct proportion to the quantum of ill deeds being committed by the followers. People are well aware of their ill-gotten riches and just as they bribe humans, they part with a small portion of this wealth to the gods. Even the poor contribute within their might to get out of poverty, illness and other problems that they face).

At this stage, an elderly devotee stood up and said "well my friends, we all agree that the temple has to be renovated. My humble suggestion is that in the name of development, we should not forget our old tradition and culture. Now we are building concrete jungles. But our temple should not be like that. We should preserve it to the maximum. So we will build an exact replica of the temple, and will not deviate from the original structure."

To this most people clapped in approval.

"Yes, sir", another man got up. "The old temple has to be an exact replica of what it looks like at present. But sirs, some parts have been ruined beyond repair. So we may have to use new material for it, but it would be exactly like the old one, using wood and masonry and clay, as was done in olden times."

"Very true" rose up another man.

Now, the vasthu and other things were decided by our forefathers' long back. Hence it would be most ideal to build the temple in this very same place, and following the exact vasthu that was being followed. (Vasthu sasthra is the traditional Indian system of architecture that originated in India).

Everybody approved this and there was a lot of murmured conversation and cross talk about the importance of vasthu, the need for following it in true spirit, the greatness of our culture and the like. After some time, the older man who first spoke, rose up again to quell the murmur and said. "My dear devotees, it has been agreed upon by all of us that the renovation has to start immediately. We already have some funds promised, and hence, we can start the demolition and renovation immediately. We will follow up with the fund raising in the coming days too. So, we will fix up the day of start of the renovation in consultation with our famous astrologer(He mentioned the name also). So, let me summarise our decisions

1.The temple will be built in the very same spot where it now stands, and following the very vasthu that it had originally.

2. To retain the history and the archeological significance, the new temple will be built as far as possible, with the very same material of the old temple in the original places where they belonged.

3. Wherever there is damage, new material will be used, but will be exactly like the old structure.

This was agreed upon by everybody. So the new temple had to be constructed at the same spot with the materials dismantled from the old temple.

Then some wise person asked how much time it will take to construct the new temple. It was estimated to take at least two years.

“In that case”, He asked. “Where will we pray during all those days, if the temple is being demolished and new construction being done”.

The meeting was about to be closed and everybody were about to leave. The salient points had already been discussed. So, some had already left. This question had come in the last minute when the majority of people had left. Then, somebody remarked from the crowd.

"Alright, we will use the present temple until the new temple is ready. Okay? "

And everybody left. That last sentence, Was the wisest, right?

Simple, logical and offering an immediate solution, isn’t it?

Now, think again. How do you keep the old temple as it is for two years, doing your worship, and at the same time dismantle it?

And also satisfy the next condition that you will use the material so dismantled for the construction of the new one at the same site, without dismantling it?

Ah, there you go. That is what we are. Too intelligent, to the level that nothing will be allowed to happen here.

So now, you must be agreeing that we are the most intelligent fools in the world. This also applies to industries, and other establishments. Consider that a factory is running into loss. What will a normal workforce do? They will work harder; more efficiently, join with the management in analyzing the loss making problems, and solve it. Sometimes, they may even forego a part of the benefits, to rescue the factory. But what happens in this state? The management may try to reduce the benefits to a small level to get out of the situation, and at the very announcement itself, many of the employees would strike work and prevent other willing workers also from running the factory. Obviously, the factory gets into deeper trouble to the point of no rescue, and eventually gets closed down and deteriorated. The workers lose their jobs, and become job seekers, with the family being ruined. From losing a little bit of money for a short time, they become permanently poor. Great logic, really. The number of establishments that we have successfully shut down, now rusting amongst bush and weed and creepers, stands as martyrs to the "intelligence" of our community.

Luckily, since we have a very good climate and good rains, it takes less than a year to cover an uncared factory to be fully covered by weeds, never to be recovered.

Welcome to Kerala, fools' own country.

CHAPTER III

Workers of the world unite, get paid for sitting Idle (the story of Nokkukooli and other wonders)

Don't get confused when you hear the new word "Nokkukooli". It is the Malayalam word for a fee to be paid to somebody for simply observing some other person/s or machinery doing work and getting paid for the work that the other person/machinery has done. You can roughly translate it as observer fee but that gives it an aura of legally valid, respectable fee, while, this nokkukooli is nothing less than broad daylight organized shameless looting. In any other part of the world, this sort of hooliganism will end you up in jail.

I will just tell you an example. You are constructing a house. For this, you need bricks, sand and a lot of other materials. You ask a tipper lorry fellow to bring one load of sand. The fellow brings it, and with the press of a button, tilts the platform and unloads it, takes his cash and pushes off. Now, in any other state, the matter ends there.

(Back ground reading ---You have to understand that in Kerala, everything is being done by groups of people who are organized into unions. In the case of loading and unloading materials from the trucks and other vehicles, there is a union called Head load workers union. They are also organized under different banners, owing allegiance to strong political parties. So, you have an established union for the leftists, one for the congress and allies, and another for the BJP. You cannot be a worker without joining any one of those unions. Now, continue your reading).

But if it is Kerala, one of any two things happens.

Situation A:

Consider that you had not informed any other fellow about your need for the sand or cement or other thing. The head load workers union in the locality will definitely get information about this load of sand that you have bought. Within a short time, be it day or night, a group of them will come to you and ask for a certain amount to be paid by you to them. You ask them why? They will explain politely, but with a little bit of sarcasm "Sir, when you unloaded this by a machine, we are losing our job. Traditionally, we used to unload the sand and other materials manually from the ordinary trucks. With the coming of these trucks with a lifting device, we are losing our job and we poor people lose our wages for a living. You have to compensate for this." If you are a first timer, you get angry and refuse to pay. Your first feeling is as though you are being robbed. You deny strongly and a verbal dual might follow depending upon your quarrelling and shouting power. Then they will threaten you and physically block every load of sand that comes to you. You will then call the police, and one or two of them may come and tell you that this is a labour dispute and they will not interfere. Normally, you will get the reply over phone itself. So, you lose the battle, and meekly surrender to their demand. Depending on the size of the lorry and the material being unloaded, the rates are different, and standardized. Mind you, this is Kerala, and everything has a rate. Even for snatchers. So, if it is a small lorry, the rate is this. For bigger ones, bigger rates. This is a democratic state, you see, where everything goes by the will of the people who decide. *(Not the will of the general public, or the law)*

Situation B.

You already have informed them about your construction . This is the second situation, where you have surrendered to the situation in Kerala. In that case, there will be somebody from the union in your site of construction, simply smoking or watching something on his mobile phone, and along with that, recording the number of loads that has been unloaded. At the end of the day, you pay him the rate based on the number of trips made. He coolly walks off to his union office, and shares this money with the other workers. *(Sorry, I said "walks off". There is a correction-- He will ride off in his bike and get to his office. Don't be astonished. Our workers are mostly well off, having at least a scooter. Thanks to the hire purchase deals of the two wheeler companies, and also the correct repayments that these workers do, most of them are in a position to afford one.)* In the case of housing projects by big builders, there is an understanding already and the "Nokkukooli" based on the number of loads unloaded is religiously remitted to the union office every evening. (There is a correction, however, that some builders have started a revolt and are not paying this). You will think that this is because of the communist rule in the state. No, all parties are involved, and all unions of all parties are birds of the same feather in doing this. After all, when money comes free, who will say no? Even their leaders, who would talk against this in public, are afraid of taking any action. It is said that there is also an unwritten agreement where the unions pay their contribution to their party every month or so. Also, when there are processions, demonstrations, Hartal, and other party activities, these people will join to make them a grand success. Mostly, the above activities are regularly entrusted to these very same workers. So, if the common public is looted, which politician will care? There is also a paradox to this. The honourable High court of Kerala, after considering a series of petitions, ordered this fleecing as an offence and instructed the police to stop this practice, wherever it is seen, and arrest the hooligans. But, as we said earlier, the policeman is also a human being, living amongst us with his family. Naturally, if these people turn against them, he will be miserable. Since these people have political support, the court orders are more ignored than observed. No policeman would risk his peaceful life for implementing the law in its true spirit.

Interestingly, a recent incidence throws light on the incapability of the court themselves in implementing their orders. There is a saying in Malayalam "bhagavane patti kadichal ithupoloru vedanayundo". Translating to English, it would mean "if the god himself is bitten by the stray dog, how will you describe the pain". The incident is like this. A judicial magistrate's office was being shifted to a new place, and the stationery and furniture was to be moved. The unloading charge demanded by the unions was Rs.18000 or so. Gov't does not pay the magistrate for this, and hence, she (it was a lady magistrate) along with her office staff, unloaded the same by themselves. This , they could do, based on another judgment of the high court that the owners of any commodity can unload their wares either by themselves or their own group. Since this was the magistrate herself doing this, the union fellows did not dare to interfere. If it was any other group, they would have prevented the unloading itself. For us Keralites, it was just interesting news in the morning papers and in television. Nobody did anything about it, even with the direct proof of the photo and video of the lady magistrate and her staff shifting the materials. If the law itself is threatened, and is helpless, what about the common people? So, this is our great "gods own country".

There is, however the other side of the story also. In doing the work allotted to them, they are quite knowledgeable, systematic, and does their job very neatly and with a technical skill. Once, I noticed that while unloading the bundle of steel rods for construction, the workers were standing in single row and almost 7 or eight of them, lifting the weight and running to the side of the truck and dropping it down. I also read a criticism about it that why this many people to unload. That question is because of ignorance about the weight of this bundle. It is very heavy, and not all workers can do this.

It is just natural for people from other places to wonder why the 35 million strong populace in Kerala, with its long tradition of fighting against oppression does not protest in their might against this injustice. For an answer, you have to know the history of Kerala for the last two or three centuries. During those times, this land which was supposedly retrieved from the sea by the saint Parasurama, was rigidly following the caste system. The Brahmins and their sub castes were the highest in social hierarchy, followed by Nairs and their sub sects. Ezhavas were in the lower rung, and the tribes were the most down trodden. The lower castes had to keep distance from the higher castes while in public places and were untouchables. The women were not allowed to cover their breasts, and lower caste people were not allowed to enter the temples, but can bow to the god from outside the temple premises. A long history of a series of agitations against these evils by social reformers became milestones of mass awakening and fight for justice. So, the might of the downtrodden was established. Workers, who had no rights, were organized, and succeeded in getting fair wages; Land was distributed from the landlords to the actual labourers, and many other reforms took place.

However, an offshoot of this awakening process was that any organized group was able to extort even unjustified demands, based on arguments and sheer muscle strength. Unfortunately, in the name of social justice, the political parties also had to support them. Kerala is the first, and probably the only state in the country, (may be the only one in the whole world) to have burnt down tractors when they were introduced. The argument was that these monsters will cause loss of work for the poor farm labourer, if they were used to plough the crop fields. The reality, that tractors were introduced due to acute shortage of labourers, was simply forgotten. Crop cultivation, especially paddy could not be done in time, and hence, whole seasons of rice cropping were abandoned. No such arguments could win during those times. But gradually, when the children of the labourers got educated and joined good paying jobs, the older generation of labourers got reduced so low, that the agitation died down on its own, and mechanization slowly gained access to the state. But, this one act against all sorts of mechanization, against the hypothetical loss of jobs, pulled back the development of the state at least by fifty years. The very same thing happened with computerization also. During the initial years, the monster, that is computer, was destroyed so ferociously, that it pulled us back again by another fifty years. Now, those people who spearheaded such agitations are using two or three laptops, PCs and all other electronic gadgets, without even an iota of shame. That is our state, Fool's own country. The populace never asks these people " are you not ashamed"? Because, the public as a lot, is gifted with the brain of a donkey (We have a saying in Malayalam, "Pothujanam kazhuthayaanu", which means exactly this). So, with all the wisdom that we have accrued over the years, the adage gets stronger: "The (Kerala) public is a Donkey". And donkeys traditionally have been patented to being fools.

Yes, we are fools own country.

CHAPTER IV

Devaluation of Indian Rupee

As we already know, Kerala is the one state in the whole country which has one hundred percent literacy. Also, it has the highest women literacy and even though I don't have the statistics, it is here that we may be having the biggest percent of Ph.Ds, doctors, engineers, IITians, master's degree holders, degree holders, matriculates and down under. This is also the only state where women outnumber males. There is also no enmity to the girl child, and in many instances, a girl is more coveted than the male child. A celestial, unbelievable panorama, right? But, is it that with the acquisition of more degrees and academic qualifications, you become more and more stupid? At least in the case of Kerala, I doubt very much.

There is a saying in Kerala which reads in Malayalam as ", avanu bhayankara buddhiya, pakshe vivaramilla"(He is very intelligent, but lacks common sense). Well, let me tell you just one example.

The story dates back to 1991.In July that year, the government of India with the Harvard Professor Dr.Manmohan Singh as the finance minister, devalued Indian rupee by a hefty 19 percent. All hell broke loose in the newspapers and economic dailies, but as they were less informed and knowledgeable than the finance minister, almost every media carried articles that described how the prices of commodities will be increased tremendously. Most of the educated elite in this part of the country, that is Kerala,read most of these articles, and in their own individualistic ego, formed the most authentic analysis of the effects of devaluation. As was customary (and still is) , every Tom, Dick and Harry in the state had his own most authentic idea about what devaluation was, why it was made and what will be its short term and long term effects on the economy and the common man. Some papers analysed that it was only the imported white good that will become costly. (Must have been near to the truth). But most intelligentsia was damn sure it will cause an increase in the cost of everyday goods. It was taken for granted. Now, let me also tell you that every small tea shop even in the remotest village of Kerala subscribes to at least one newspaper . The barber shop is another place where you also get weeklies, cinema magazines etc.. So these are places where people go to read the news. In some places, there is an arrangement where one person reads the news and others hear it. There will be responses to some of the news items, and later, elaborate discussions, based on some of the top news. And, without his morning news our morning tea is not complete. So even the ordinary man is aware of local, national and even international news. Don't underestimate us.

Now, coming to the real story. There was a small "all goods shop" just outside the residential quarters that were given to the teachers of the Kerala Agricultural University.(Those days, I was one among the faculty) . This shop had groceries, vegetables, cigarettes and almost all things that the family needed. Local people always bought their everyday needs from this shop. The teachers also shopped here, but were not exclusively dependant on him. In the days after devaluation also, many of the knowledgeable people like Professors and clerks went to this shop and purchased items. The shopkeeper was wise enough to cash in on the newsfeed about the devaluation that he got from the morning newspapers and had arbitrarily increased the prices. All of the well-read, educated customers didn't question the price rise, because they also had read the papers. They were hence aware that devaluation will cause higher prices. Some, of them however did question. And the shopkeeper deftly replied-"sir, don't you know the rupee has been devalued. So, how can I give for the lower price?" And they all again were enlightened and walked off, paying the higher price.

Later in the evening, one of the regular customers came. This man was Palanichami, a migrant worker from neighboring Tamil Nadu. He was illiterate and a common worker. He will work till evening and get a wage of 300 or so. Almost half of it, he will spend in the liquor shop for his drinks and customary additional eateries. Then he will, as a responsible husband and father, take home the provisions for the next day. This consisted of a kilogram of rice, little gram, chillies, onion , oil, and the like. The price range and all was known to both Palanichami and Kuttappan, the shop owner. So Kuttappan will total the cost of all and tell the amount. Palani, on his side will pay him whatever was left in his hand after what he paid in the liquor shop. Some days, there will be a shortage of 10 or 15 rupees, but by the end of the week, whatever was due, will be cleared by Palani by cutting on his liquor quota or some other adjustment. This was going on for a long time among the two. This day, the shopkeeper gave an amount which was about 50 Rs. more than normal. Palanichami enquired why this hike came. To this, Kuttappan, very scornfully, mocking at the latter's ignorance, declared in Tamil, palanichami's native language. " *Annachee, rupaayude vila kammi panniyach. Pathrikayile vandirundathu.Neenge padikkaleya. Athinale vela eri poyachu"*(Brother, the price of the rupee has been reduced. It was there in the newspapers. Didn't you read? So, the prices have increased.) Even though he was slightly drunk, this man couldn't digest this great economics. For him, nothing had changed.

He took a few moments to compose himself, and without any provocation, went straight to Kuttappan and slapped him on both cheeks firmly. After which he spoke thus. " *yen ..da, rupayude vela eppadi kammi panniyathu. Netru intha mootayil iruntha arisi thane innekkum irikkathu.Athe milaku, athe paruppu, venkayam, karuvadu.Nan netru kodutha mathiri athe rupaa than innekum koduppathu.Yenda nan antha rupayude side cut panneetingala? Appo eppadi da roopayude vela kammi varathu ?*"(Why ,mister? How was the rupees' value reduced? You are selling the very same rice that was left in this sack yesterday. That very same chilli, red gram, onion and dry fish. I am giving you the rupee notes that are exactly like the ones that I gave you yesterday. Did I cut the sides of the notes and am giving you the cut sized notes? So how is it that the value of the rupee is reduced).

Kuttappan was thunderstruck at the very simple logic that he failed to get from the so called very literate, elite customers that he had fooled till now. Instantaneously, he went back to the old rates for illiterate customers like Palanichami.

In a way, it is also a blessing to be ignorant, is it??

And we pride ourselves in being fools own country

CHAPTER V

How we solve our problems in Kerala - Finding the man-eater tiger in the forest

Many of you would have read the book"Man-Eaters of Kumaon". This is a 1944 book written by hunter-naturalist Jim Corbett. It details the experiences that Corbett had in the Kumaon region of India from the 1900s to the 1930s, while hunting man-eating Bengal tigers and Indian leopards.

Our story is about what would have happened in a situation if such a man eater was to be captured in various countries/ places in various parts of the world.

Situation 1. Say if it happened in Europe.

They have a liking for solving problems in the way of Sherlock Holmes. The government came to know about the tiger that has turned to a man eater and is hiding in the forest. So, just in Sherlock Holmes style, a set of experts were briefed on the whereabouts of the tiger and they were entrusted with the job of catching it. And, the small team leaves for the forest, with their essentials, including food. Until they reach the scene, they are playing cards or otherwise enjoying, since, they don't gain anything by discussing on something that they don't know more about, other than the briefing that they got. Once in the scene of the man eater, they gather as much information from local people and other sources about the whereabouts of the tiger. Then, without any huss or fuss, they found out the tiger's location and set traps and also night vision points atop high trees and stayed there. They had already tracked the path of the tiger as much as possible, and in a day or two, the tiger is either caught in the trap or net or is killed by gunshot. They come back and return to their duty.

Situation 2. Say if it happened in America

Things happen in typical Hollywood style. Of course, there would be briefing. But there will be theatrical drama, with some in the team dissenting, some inside quarrel, a dog squadron, and a team, with a pretty girl and a handsome guy, along with others. They hover over the site by helicopter, and will have the back up of a whole army of supersonic jets and computer controlled damage control mission. The lady and the gun trotting men will cover the wild complete with waterfalls, all sorts of wild creatures and all that, and ultimately catch the tiger. However, in the fight, they will lose some of their most trustworthy men and will be leaving a lot of destruction just behind the lady and her accomplice, both with bruises and blood stained faces etc. However, the search ends in a positive note, and the tiger is caught.

Situation 3.Be it Israel.

They would take off with a set of commandos and, in typical Entebbe style, finish off the leopard in no time, and wouldn't even bother to bury the corpse or make a photo session of it, but would allow the jungle to process the corpse in its own natural way.

Situation 4 :If it was in India, other than Kerala

A whole crowd of villagers would chase the whole forest with sticks and stones, but would ultimately kill the man eater, maybe, with some minor bruises for the participants.

Situation 4 :Now, once this happened in Kerala.

There was a man-eater tiger, and it was necessary to catch it or kill it. And four or five teams were formed to do the job and all of them set out into the jungle. Weeks passed, but the man-eater was not caught, but its menace continued. Unable to wait any longer, the government sent search teams by Helicopter into the jungle. What they could see was at least three different groups who had a bear, a lion and a gorilla each in their custody. Each of these teams were thrashing these poor animals left and right, asking them to confess that the animal they had caught was indeed the man-eater tiger. That's how we deal with problems.

They are never solved, but are pretended to be solved, with tall claims and cacophony, but it remains there eternally. That's us, the great Keralite. This you have to read along with the next chapter -" Enthosulfan-the maker of all evils". Twenty five years after the last drop of this chemical

Endosulfan was sprayed anywhere in the whole of Kerala, the disorders and diseases continue in those very same populations. We still accuse the insecticide for the continued occurrence of health disorders and would not allow the real cause to be investigated.

We love to remain ourselves as fools' own Country

CHAPTER VI

Enthosulfan-the maker of all evils

Enthosulfan-the maker of all evils (Warning: This chapter, because of the inherent technical nature of the content, would require some serious reading and hence, to an extent, make it tough prose)

I have put the title as "enthosulfan", specifically because, "entho" in Malayalam means something that we don't really know.

Read the next conversation "What did he say?" "I don't really know. (in Malayalam) Entho paranju "(said something that I didn't understand).

So,enthosulfan means some sulfan that I dont know.

Endosulfan, the insecticide, was in a similar way, to the press and the general public, just "entho sulfan"-some sulfan they didn't know.

But all of them believed that all the maladies in Padre near Kasargod were caused by this so called "---sulfan". All of them believed this blindly, believed, even though every argument that was put forth against Endosulfan was also against sheer common sense. That is why I testify that all Keralites or at least the majority of us, are fools.

In Mahabharata, there is an instance when Parasurama the saint and guru of Karna, cursed him that when he needed it most, Karna will forget his knowledge and mastery of weapon use. This is the type of forgetfulness that forms the basis of the world famous foolishness of us Keralites. Let us now refresh our memory of this malady. In 2001, three news reports and a series of follow up news painted the tragic fate of poor souls in Padre, a remote village in Kasargod district of Kerala, **suffering from various deformities, a high prevalence of cancers of different organs, neurological disorders like epilepsy,cerebral palsy, psychiatric disorders, congenital malformations and reproductive problems, asthma and skin diseases during the previous 10 years. To emphasize the malady, photos of the suffering souls with mental retardation, super sized head, atrophied body parts and lots of other ailments were also published.**

Anybody with a little bit of kindness in heart would easily feel disturbed by these photos, and without any further questions asked, believe fully that the tragedy was due to Endosulfan. It is natural that when you believe the first part of the story with the photos of the poor souls, you naturally tend to believe the second part also. Through a campaign that took the intelligentsia for granted, it was sealed in the minds of people that Endosulfan, an insecticide sprayed by helicopters caused irreparable health hazards to a hapless population in Padre, the obscure village in Kasargod district of Kerala. The press, the politicians, and the common man, allowed this to be instilled in their mind as the curse and injustice that was perpetuated onto a population of illiterate,helpless poor villagers. Doubtless, this attracted media attention worldwide and anybody who could pose to have first-hand access to information from the village got a lot of media coverage. Stories were manufactured and ultimately ended up in the unscientific and unjustified banning of some very useful, cost effective pesticides .These were some of the cheapest chemicals for crop management, but sadly had to be replaced by very costly substitutes, putting a lot of financial strain on the poor farmer. Anybody who tried to expose this falsehood and to bring the real facts into limelight, were branded as anti-poor, anti-social and anti-empathy and also to be bribed by the multinational insecticidal lobby. Doubtless to say, their tongues were tied,and all of them had to make a hasty retreat. There is another paradox to it. **Most of the Endosulfan in India was being manufactured by a central government organization, The Hindustan insecticides Limited. It was obvious they would never offer bribes to government officials.** But, as Mark twain remarked **"A lie can travel half way around the world, while the truth is putting on its shoes"**

Now, let us come to the bare facts or ground realities about the Endosulfan spray. The problem started with the spraying of pesticides in the cashew plantations of the Plantation corporation of Kerala,or PCK , a body under the Government of Kerala. As in the case of any other corporation, PCK also is not really a one hundred percent under government department. Unfortunately, just as in Government, PCK also would be having its own inherent red tapes, corruption wherever possible, plus all other evils a government agency has. The issue is regarding the spraying of Endosulfan in the cashew estate located in padre in Kasargod.

This estate is having an area of only about 60 ha. The total area of cashew belonging to PCK in the state of Kerala is around **5000Ha.**

The split up is

Alakode estate 80 Ha

Cheemeni 856 Ha

Kasargod 2190 Ha

Rajapuram 1523 Ha

The above information is from the company website, which gives the description that it has **6361 Ha** under cashew and gave the split up as above. However, this adds to only **5193 Ha**. This itself speaks volumes about the efficiency of the corporation,right??? And the wonderful way they keep records of their own land holdings. **And you accept that this corporation with this track record of even not knowing their own land possessions, had meticulously sprayed all these 5000-6000 ha thrice a year, for 20 years or more with the very same insecticide?**

Are you not a fool of the first order to believe that they did?

Again,the padre plot is only around 60 ha. When you accuse the PCK that they sprayed this enthosulfan for 20 years continuously , thrice an year in the meekly 60 Ha in Padre village in Kasargod, what else can I describe you other than as "the most literate, intelligent fool in the world"???

So, come friends, let us declare ourselves as fools own country.

One more reason to disbelieve the 20 year 3 times theory is the location of Padre. The 60 ha in padre is under the Muliyar estate, and is situated in isolation about 28 kilometers from the main estate in Muliyar. As per record (and as per the propaganda unlcashed by the pronouncers of the manmade disaster theory), spraying of this pesticide has been done in all estates under PCK, for around 20 years. (Unfortunately, PCK cannot deny that, because, probably, their records would have shown a systematic purchase of the pesticide all these years and any denial would reveal the corruption, if any). Except in this 60 Ha area of Padre, no other area in the total of more than 6000 Ha has complained about any such health hazards in the population. Any right thinking person would have immediately written off the Endosulfan theory, and would have tried to investigate the real cause. But, in Kerala, as I said earlier, we are stubborn to the core, and just as in the story that I mentioned earlier, trying to make the poor bear accept that indeed, it is the man eater leopard.

Again, I will give you some more facts.

Normally, if you mentioned that PCK sprayed this pesticide religiously in their entire cashew estates thrice an year for 20 years in all their cashew estates, the Keralite would laugh at you. Because, they know for sure, that such a thing can never happen in a government owned corporation. That spraying is subject to the commission by all the intermediaries, and in the far off , least populated dry , unapproachable cashew estates of PCK, nobody would even venture once, to verify the occurrence of spraying. But in this case, the so called saviours of the downtrodden in Padre Village say it happened, and all those who questioned it in their minds, simply swallowed their doubts. So they believe PCK did this all those years.

There is also another fact. PCK does not own a helicopter and so they cannot spray their chemicals as and when they please.It is always hired from North India, usually from Punjab. The copter is dismantled, and transported to Kerala. It is reassembled here, and after the spraying schedule, dismantled and sent back, again, by truck. Any verification of the records would easily reveal how many times the copter was hired, and for cashew, specifically. (The PCK also sprays for Rubber in its estates using Helicopter, for preventing leaf disease). Unfortunately, when all these records were readily available, nobody ever cared to verify them, but instead, simply believed the exaggerations, and not even tried to correlate **the cause effect relationship.** The estate at padre does not have a helipad, and hence, the copter flies after loading the pesticide from the Helipad at Muliyar to this estate at Padre and comes back. The distance by road is 28 Km, and aerial distance must be around 15 Km. In state run PCK, do you believe the helicopter went this distance, thrice an year, for 20 years? "Fools of the world, unite. You have nothing to lose other than your brain ".

Let us also try to understand the scientific evidence. The symptoms expressed in the population at Padre, was never systematically recorded, and surveys specifically to arrive at the reasons were never done. The NIOH, the National institute of Occupational Health, under the Indian Council of Medical Research , had conducted a survey in the area, and published its report. It is this report that is very often quoted by the protagonists of the Endosulfan malady. **It is definite that these people have never read the report, because that report categorically and sarcastically disproves many of the claims raised by the propagandists.** According to the NIOH, the total area under cashew for PCK totals 4715 Ha, while PCK in its website says it has 6361 Ha under cashew and gave the split up which adds to only 5193 Ha. This report, in very clear terms, **has castrated the**

claims of the doctor who opened up the Pandora's box pertaining to the Endosulfan cruelty. He was the one who very intelligently observed that his patients from one side of his village were affected and patients from the other side were free. So, in Sherlock Holmes style, he investigated and pinned the crime on Endosulfan. He was too eager to proclaim his prize information to the world (may be also because he had no knowledge about the basic rules of a scientific study and its validation) and to fulfill his social obligation. As a sequel to the propaganda unleashed in the media, a Delhi based NGO also, supposedly collected blood samples from the affected population, and conducted quantitative estimation of residues and published stunning and insinuating results in their house magazine, "Down to Earth". And not surprisingly, many of the other media also quoted this as authentic information, and fomented the fire. The NIOH study, even though was not systematic and comprehensive, still made a dig on the reported content of Endosulfan in the samples of the test population published by CSE. They exposed the inherent drawbacks in the aforesaid study with just one expose. That is, in other parts of the world, where, in accidental deaths due to this Endosulfan, the levels in blood were only 4-8 parts per million or ppm, the CSE study reports Endosulfan levels to be as high as 108-196 ppm in the blood samples of the persons they surveyed. **Which means, that if they really had this much high levels, they should have died years back, and if they are still alive, What we see now are supernatural humans , walking dead.**

(This report was probably not much read and discussed by the world scientific bodies, because otherwise, all the medical research teams and pesticide researchers around the world would have rushed to Padre to scientifically study these super humans for their wonderful resistance capacity and to get at least some stem cells from these people, to build a superhuman race that could even drink pesticides and walk coolly on earth. So unfortunate for us, Indians!!!!!)

(See page 6 from the NIOH report."CSE Study: Quantitative estimation of Endosulfan levels in biological and environmental samples was done by a very sensitive and sophisticated technique called gas chromatography equipped with the ECD detector. This technique although very sophisticated for quantitative estimation, cannot identify an unknown substance, which needs to be confirmed

by using standard tests. This was particularly essential because the investigators reported the levels of Endosulfan varying between 108 and 196 ppm in the blood of all subjects with varying degrees of illnesses. These levels are much higher than the reported blood levels of 4-8 ppm in three fatal Endosulfan poisoning cases (Coutselinis A., Kentarchou E and Boukis D. 1978 Concentration level of endosulfan in biological material (Report of three cases) Forensic Sc. 11:75) and 2.9 ppm in another case of fatal Endosulfan poisoning (Blanco-Coronado JL Repetto M Geinestal RJ et al, 1992. Acute intoxication by endosulfan J Clin Toxicol 30:575-583.).

No attempt was made by the investigator to confirm the presence of Endosulfan.That is, when people in other countries had 4-8 ppm in their blood, they died. But here, with 108 to 196 ppm poison in their blood, these superhumans are walking coolly on the streets of Padre. How wonderful?? There are, however, many reports, conducted routinely as part of the health surveys that very authentically state that the levels of the maladies reported in Kasargod, are lower than in some other districts, which had never been sprayed by Endosulfan. However, these reports are never seriously taken by the wonderfully intelligent Keralite. Ha Ha Ha.!!!!

In the name of the catastrophe, the state governed has spent crores of rupees from the state fund, just as compensation for the victims of the spray. How wonderful? Even accidental deaths would have been accounted in this category and compensation given.

There is an interesting addendum to this whole episode which most players in the field have never known and were unknowingly playing into the hands of a strong illegal lobby of multinationals who wanted Endosulfan to be banned. Here is why. Endosulfan was one of the cheapest insecticides available in the market. It is toxic to fish, but is relatively safe to pollinating bees. It is for this reason that this chemical was recommended for the first spray in cashew, coinciding with the flowering. Many bees come during this season, and in and around cashew plantations, this is the honey flow season. So, even though you spray Endosulfan, the bees are safe, but the cashew flowers are protected. As in the case of any product, Endosulfan was also being manufactured under license from the original patent holders, but patent rights of Endosulfan expired in 2005 or so, after being in force for 50 years. This meant that anybody in any country can simply produce and sell this in their market, without giving even a penny to the original patent holder. India and china were the largest producers of this cheap pesticide. So, they could sell this all over the world including the poor countries in

Africa and other regions. However, because this was very cheap, it will be a big competitor to its very costly substitutes manufactured by other companies.

In India, the largest manufacturers were Hindustan Insecticides Limited, a company owned by the Govt. of India and Excel industries. No other bigger companies in our country were manufacturing this product. So, why should other pesticide manufacturers fight for a product that they never produce? Again, the mainstream produces in the pesticide industry had very costly, very specific, newer substitutes to sell, and a support for Endosulfan would mean that endosulfan is freely available. What they wanted was the ban, because, once that is done, all these companies have newer products that act only specifically, and were much costlier than the old peasticide. if one pesticide is specific,it means that for every pest, you have to use specific insecticide. So, the pesticide industry, in India or elsewhere never made any concentrated efforts to counter the misinformation. Every manufacturer played a silent spectator role, but the ultimate loser was the Govt. of India and the poor farmer who always had no choice other than to buy the costly substitutes. The ultimate result of the ban on Endosulfan and other low cost broad acting chemicals was that third world countries lost their cheap pesticides.They will pay heavily for the very specific acting,"environment friendly" pesticides that does not act on any other organism other than the target species. All of them were produced by multinationals and will be adding to their profits year after year. Banning of broad acting pesticides means that the farmer will have to use a dozen specific pesticides which are damn costly, for tackling the different pests in the crop. These costly pesticides are undoubtedly more environment friendly, but the farmer sprays more number of very costly chemicals, instead of one general pesticide. **This means that the farmer's pocket is pilfered, and snatches the meager profit from the food bowl of the wretched farmer in the third world, for the luxuries of the lavishly rich.**

Also understand that when you combine the residues of all the different pesticides that the farmer was forced to spray to kill the many pests in his field, will the combined residue be lower than that of the old single dose pesticide? Use your brain if you have one.

Before I end up with this note, I would suggest that at least some impartial people from the press or media should visit the site in Padre and find out how much of the land as per records is in real possession of PCK.

And, as an offshoot, did it also lose its property to land grabbers?

Were we not made fools of the first order?

Welcome to fools own country

CHAPTER VII

Save our Rivers –Stop sand mining

This is another of the wonderful bright ideas that was invented, propagated and successfully implemented by us, the great fools. The history of this starts with the sanding of our rivers. (This word sanding is a new addition to the English language by me. There is a similar word, very popular in ecology related descriptions. That word is "SILTING", which means the addition of silt, usually in the dams, river sides and other areas related to flowing water. The word meaning is "the process of adding silt, the fine soil particles that get carried along with the flowing water, especially after torrential rains that rake up the top soil and carries the fine particles along with it, and deposits it downstream, somewhere". (So, in a similar fashion, if sand is carried by the river and is deposited in the lower reaches of a river, what better word to connote it than SANDING? Am I not right???)

Why did sanding occur?

You know, we Keralites are explorers by gene. You would have heard of Pilgrim Fathers who left England and landed up in America and established the present USA. But they are confined to that place, and do not move out to other countries, usually. The Keralite, on the other hand, is a natural nomad, seeking greener pastures day in and day out. You won't have a place on earth, where a Keralite is not there. A very common sarcastic, but also envious comment about us Keralites is that when **Edmund Hillary and Tenzing Norgay** reached mount Everest, on the way, **they met a Keralite, running a Nair's tea shop**. The experience of Neil Armstrong and Michel Collins might have been no different in the moon. !!! Back on earth, in our own state, people from Travancore, especially Kottayam and adjoining areas had a tendency to move to the western ghats hills and conquer the land. They are called by the sweet pet name, Settlers, meaning, they settled from somewhere to this new place. They came to the hilly areas of Malabar, the erstwhile Madras state, may be about 70-80 years back. Those days, Malabar had the feudal system, and most of the lands were with the tenants. The land owners got "paattam" or a seasonal rent in kind. When the Kerala Land Reforms amendment act came in 1969, much of this land that were tenancy lands were automatically declared as excess lands above the land ceiling limit. All those lands went to the government as property in excess of the allowable acreage, and many of these uncared for land was encroached by these settlers. Many also ventured into the forest land, that was adjoining to this .

Initially, the first thing that these people used to do was to cut the trees in the land and make a small hut out of that. Then the remaining trees and all other vegetation are cut, and the logs sold. The rest is used as firewood.

{you: "Hey buddy, are you going to talk about rivers, or settlers or sanding? Come to the point".

Me: "Sir, if you have to know what caused sanding, you have to know what caused the sand to get filled in the river. I am explaining. Be patient. Kindly continue reading"}.

The next step is to plough the whole place and plant tapioca. Tapioca has the unique distinction of not being eaten by the wild animals, because tapioca contains a poisonous chemical, Hydrocyanic acid or HCN, and can be removed only by boiling and draining off the boiled water . The toxin gets dissolved in the water and is removed. They will also plant rubber alongside, and some banana, if the wild animals permit them to grow it. Many of them also had country made guns, which they used to frighten the wild animals and also to hunt small animals like wild hare, pigs etc. This meat was used to cook as fresh meat and the balance was dried in the rocky terrain to be used later on in the rainy season etc. They were real fighters, fighting with the rocky terrain, with not much of vehicular connection, and scarce medical attention available nearby. The surrounding population was also meagre until with the passing of time, other people of the same genre came in. By and by, these forest lands got converted to farmlands, and large scale cultivation caused a lot of forests to be destroyed. Most of these people also belonged to the Christian community, and within a short time, they would erect a small Christian chapel atop the hill, and start Sunday prayers. These people also had a connection with the political parties and were hence, a large vote bank. So, naturally, the politicians turned a blind eye to these encroachments. This was the situation that occurred in the 1940-1975 period. This settler syndrome was initially confined to areas near Calicut district, and then got spread to other northern districts and even to the interiors of Karnataka beyond Mangalore. They all thrive there still. Because of the political clout, successive governments gave in to the demand of these settlers to get "pattayaas" or title deeds for the land they encroached. Over the passage of time, the cut off year for forest encroachment to be validated by pattayas got extended. In other words, the land that belonged to some old landlord or was the government forest land became legal property of these intruders. This legalization of encroached land was done at frequent intervals. Every time, due to the hue and cry and political pressure, this date continues to be extended, so that encroachments about 10 years back also have a chance to be legalized. I do not know what the current cutoff date is, but am sure that it will get extended to more recent years as the years pass by. Everything said and done, the end result was that the forests were denuded, new highland settlements and city life got established in hills, and life flourished.

The only drawback was that the forest cover got depleted. Seasons of rain and shine got changed. But the cultivation of tapioca and rubber and other soil ploughing over many years caused extensive soil erosion. The top soil got washed away and went into the ocean, fertilizing the ocean with the organic rich humus. In the run off, the sand particles (which are heavier) got carried away to lower reaches, and over the years, got transported to the lower plains of the rivers. With nowhere else to go beyond, these sand particles became sand dunes in many rivers.

Now, the second part about sanding, that was the prime aim of this chapter.

During he past 30 years or so, there was big construction boom going on in the state, particularly after many of the nomadic Keralites got a foothold in the gulf countries, and started sending money to the home state. And, the Keralite has a penchant for building palatial homes. In even remote villages, large mansions came up. Construction work boomed like anything, and cement, sand, steel, and all building materials were in great demand. Now, this sand, which got accumulated in the rivers, was one source for meeting the demand for sand. Much of the sand dunes were in Bharathapuzha, the biggest river in the state. This was freely available on the dry river bed, nd people could simply dig it out and transport to the sites. In other rivers, it was deposited down below on the riverbed, and had to be excavated by expert swimmers. They dived into the riverbed with baskets and spade, and brought it up in baskets. This they deposited in small canoes stationed above the water. This was then marketed as river sand.

When these things were happening, another particular character of the Keralite surfaced. This is called as the crab syndrome. Every one of us has this capacity, innately woven into our blood. There is even a story behind this. A person from outside Kerala while on a visit to this fools' own country, wanted to collect some crabs. He got the help of a local fisherman and started collecting crabs. The fisherman was collecting the crabs and putting them in an open vessel. The curious outsider asked why the crabs were not covered with a lid. They would be escaping, is it not? The fisherman answered. "You don't know them. They are Kerala crabs. If one tries to escape, all others will pull him down. So, none can escape, that's us". So then, many of us crabs had to find out a reason to prevent some fellows making money out of this sand. For this, a new name was coined for the process, for ease of use. We called it sand mining, to bring in as much horror as though it was something as horrendous, risky, anti-earth activity similar to the - deep down the earth- coal mining. All sorts of ecological backlashes were professed, and this propaganda clicked. The removal of river sand was regulated by the government. Mind you, this single legislation on prevention of the treacherous sand mining opened up a million opportunities for corruption. Where there is a law, there will be lawbreakers and there will be underground deals between the officials earmarked for the implementation of the law and the operators who do against it. So, in this case, the village panchayats, and other officials of the local self-government were to issue passes for sand mining. The police would verify the pass, and the whole chain of corruption got established in no time. The cost of the sand skyrocketed, considering the risks, the payment of fees and other associated expenses. With one pass, many loads of sand were transported, and intermediary hands were always bribed. Some foolish officers, who were very upright and who stood against the corruption were transferred in very short time. In the operation mode for illegal transport of sand, there will be pilot vehicles like motorbikes or so, who will give intimation about police checks etc., and the whole game continues till this day.

But now a day, a new substance has replaced river sand, and that is M sand or granite dust in short. Because of this, another form of destruction of the hills is taking place. Large hills are blasted and with heavy machinery, the rock is powdered and sold as sand.

In a short period of time, you will not see the Western Ghats at all, but you can simply see Tamil Nadu from Kerala without the obstruction of the hills.

The argument given against removal of sand from the rivers is one great example of how we could be better fools than the "birbal fools". Stop killing the river – was the slogan. With just one stroke, we malayalees ensured a slow death for both the river and the western ghat hills. No sand will be removed, the rivers will be choked, and the hills will be powdered to just sand making factories, ultimately converting hills into plain lands. If you go to Bharathapuzha, you can see kilometer stretches of sand dunes, and also, small island like formations in the middle of the river. Many of these are with luxuriant weed growth, and some have been converted to shrub jungle. This of course, kills the sand. But here, I should be cautious. Because, if some wise environmentalist hears about this shrub jungle, they will shout that "see, we had been saying that preventing sand mining will save the river. You see, there is forest in the midst of the river. What else can you expect than this wonderful saving of the river?" There is a saying that you cannot argue and educate an ignorant person or somebody who is posing to be ignorant. So, I give up.

Now, the most important fact is that there is absolutely no scientific evidence that removal of sand from the riverbed will kill the river. On the contrary, it is the reverse that is true. Every person well versed with the characters of soil, know that sand is one particle which has the least capacity to hold water. It is the humus, clay and other finer particles that has a better capacity to hold water

Available Water Capacity by Soil Texture	
Textural Class	Available Water Capacity (Inches/Foot of Depth)
Coarse sand	0.25–0.75
Fine sand	0.75–1.00
Loamy sand	1.10–1.20
Sandy loam	1.25–1.40
Fine sandy loam	1.50–2.00
Silt loam	2.00–2.50
Silty clay loam	1.80–2.00
Silty clay	1.50–1.70
Clay	1.20–1.50

Just understand how much water sand can hold

So, ideally, the sand that gets deposited in the river should have been removed immediately, and the river allowed to flow with its original soil bed, so that the water flows freely. Then the soil will get soaked, and the water will percolate down, thus increasing the water availability and bringing up the water table in the nearby areas. By allowing the river sand to get accumulated, the sand absorbs all the water, and does not allow it to flow. When the rain water flow stops, there are the sun's rays, and the water captured inside the sand dunes gets evaporated from there itself. So, there is no water available downstream, and the river loses its water. It turns out dry within a few days. That is what we do, we intelligent fools. This can easily be demonstrated also.

Do this and find out if sand in rivers saves the river or kills it

Take two long plastic gutter channels and fill one with silty soil and the other with sand. Allow a thin line of water to flow from one end to the other in both and see how much time it takes for the water to reach the other end. You will see that the sand filled gutter channel takes more time and absorbs more water. Now, stop the flow and leave it in the sun. The sand channel will lose all its water in a few hours, but the other one will be wet for days. So, do you keep the sand in the river or remove it? All these scientific facts would be accepted by the ordinary people. But we are a wise lot, who continue to capture the first bear that comes across us, and beat it up continuously for days on end,(and in this case, for years together, repeating the rhetoric) to accept that it is the man-eating tiger. The least we can do is to allow the sand to be excavated and used. We should also reduce quarrying to the least necessary and use alternate technologies to construct buildings . But No. We will never do it.

We are a wonderful lot of great fools.

Welcome to fools own country

CHAPTER VIII

Five Mondays and five sundays in February

At least for this story, I am happy that there are lots of our own kith and kin of fools around the globe. We are not alone on this planet on being an accredited fool. Of course, in some other instances also, we have our brethren fools in many parts of the world.

This is about a message that got wide circulation in social media like Whatsapp and Facebook. This was with reference to the number of Mondays Tuesdays Wednesdays etc. in the month of February. It read like this.

"This February cannot come in your lifetime again. Because this year February has 4 Sundays, 4 Mondays, 4 Tuesdays, 4 Wednesdays, 4 Thursdays, 4 Fridays and 4 Saturdays. This happens once every 823 years. This is called money bags."Please forward this to as many of your friends as fast as you can and you will be rewarded for every forward. The earliest will get the maximum moneybags.

Needless to say , before they really read the message, many around the globe forwarded it to as many friends as they can, and the original person/ firm who invented the foolish prose, got the address of as many fools as they could, to be sold later to prospective customers for marketing their products. But, just think. This is something that happens every year. Every February has 28 days. When divided by 7 days a week that equals 4 of each day... 4 Sundays, 4 Mondays, 4 Tuesdays, 4 Wednesdays, 4 Thursdays, 4 Fridays and 4 Saturdays. Thus, when you see the 823 years and all, you simply fall for it without ever thinking a bit about it, and then forward it. Thus, you add your name in the number of fools in the world.

Facebook has a habit if reminding about your past activity. So has Google. They churn out what you have done before, may be a year later or so, and when you see it, you again post it, making yourself a second time fool, unless you understood your folly in between. April 1 is International fool's day. With the advent of social media, it seems that we have to declare

February as "International fool's month". The above version or a still modified version is also doing the rounds. The modified version says that this February you will have 5 Mondays, 5 Tuesdays etc.. and happens only once in 823 years. Again, you are a fool if you forward it. Actually, the original post must have originated in 2016, because, 2016 was a leap year and had 29 days. The first of February was a Monday, and due to this, that year, there were five Mondays in that month. Everybody would know that in a leap year, with 29 days in February, there would be one extra day for one week, which will repeat five times that month. It's simple. 7 days x4= 28, plus one extra day, making the total to 29 days. If the month starts on a Tuesday, there will be five of Tuesdays, and if it was on any other day, that day will come 5 times, say Thursday, Friday Saturday etc. But the post was very peculiar. It said that this year, we have 5 Mondays, 5 Tuesdays, 5 Wednesdays, 5 Thursdays, five Fridays, five Saturdays and five Sundays. Mind you, if you take the number of people who forwarded it, you will be astonished by the number of highly educated fools amidst us. You have not even thought about the simple mathematics that if there were five SMTWTFS in a month, the total number of days in that month should be 5x7=35 days. Has anybody come across a Gregorian calendar that has 35 days in any of its months?

There were two hidden agenda to make a further fool of you. One was that such a unique phenomenon happens only once in 823 years. So, you get doubly fooled, and in your eagerness to share this wonderful finding, you don't even read the whole thing, and shares it with many people. They, in turn repeat the very same error, and a large chain of fools get accumulated worldwide. The second catch is that if you share it in the next five minutes to 5 people, you will get this fortune, and if it were to 10 people, this greater fortune and the like. What actually happens is that you are, unwittingly sending the address of your acquaintances to the site that planted the story. Other ulterior motives may be there, but for that, ask a cyber-expert.

Now, can I ask you a question? How many months have 28 days in it?

If your answer was one, pertaining to February, please join the bandwagon of fools. Because every month in the calendar has 28 or 28+ days!!!!!! So there are 12 moonths in an year which has 28 days.

Well, we are a fools' own country

CHAPTER IX

Nagapushpam or Pennatulacea

This is another example of the wonderful campaigning power of we fools malayalees. Some time back, this was in circulation in social media and anybody with some intuition gave various explanations and attributes to this photo.

The photo of Nagapushpam as was publicised

Everything originated when some wise guy came across this picture. His imagination made him to think that the photo resembles the expanded hood of a cobra, but this was definitely not a cobra, but resembles a beautiful flower. So, that person designated it as Nagapushpa., which meant a cobra -like flower. Then, somebody who read it took the imagination to a further level and declared it as " **Nagapushpa flower which blooms only once in 36 yrs. It bloomed today at 3:30AM at Manasarovar Himalayas"**. Actually, you can read what it is, from below

"Some call it a Nagapushpam because it looks like a hooded snake. Actually this is a marine species (=found in the sea) called sea pens or Pennatulacea. Sea pens are all colonial, marine species. They have earned the name because many species, but certainly not all, look like an antique quill pen. There are multiple polyps on each colony, and each polyp has eight arms, as one should expect from a member of the subclass Octocorallia. In contrast to other octocorals, the polyps of sea pens specialize to perform specific tasks, like feeding or reproduction. All colonies have a central stem."

Some more information from the internet gave the description as

"However, this photograph does not depict any type of flower or plant; it was taken in 2013 by Gordon J. Bowbrick, who identified the pictured creature as a sea pen, a marine invertebrate known as an anthozoan: This creature is indeed related to anenomes and the soft corals. Sea Pens — Pennatulacea. They have the ability to pull themselves down into the reef and vanish if threatened. You can see the tube like structure at the base. Hard to see at this size but there are also a number of small cleaner shrimp in the photo close to the central quill of the feather".

As you would now know, the name sea pen was given to this type of sea living plants because they resemble the feather like part of a quill pen. (For those of you who are young and have never heard of or seen aquill pen, *"A quill pen is a dip and write pen, that was one of the first writing instruments of mankind"*. In olden days, people wrote with these pens, by dipping in a bottle of ink, and periodically replenishing the ink by dipping again in the ink bottle. The new generation of people would have never come to know about a quill pen. They have, in their earlier years, come across the fountain pen, and the still younger would have used the dot pen. These days, people don't write at all, and they have some stick to write on an electronic panel, be it the cell phone, or I pad or the like. Otherwise, they type on their computers. For ease of understanding, I am giving here the picture of a quill pen and ink bottle. Of course, I got it by google - ing.)

A quill pen

Now, coming back to us fools, this person who named the picture as Nagapushpa asked the reader to worship this for pleasing the snake gods and to bring in wealth to the home and protection from snakes and all sorts of imaginary things that he could pen at that time. Others took over from where that person left, and stated that this one is blooming in the top ranges of the Himalayas and blooms only once in 265 years (or 123 or 1033 or 4654 years or whatever figure that came in handy for them)and so, you will never get a second chance to view this in your life time. Hence, you have to send it to as many people as possible to get as much benefit that can accrue out of it. If you don't do it, you lose this opportunity and hence, will not become rich and blessed in all ways.

Without reading it again, most of we wise men immediately started sharing it so that they join the bandwagon of fools at the earliest. **If the benevolence is withdrawn at any time, due to a demand- supply gap, they didn't want to be left lurching in the wild!!!!.** These people did not have even a second's relaxation to think, and to understand that it is there in the internet, and as long as the internet exists, you can always retrieve it any time of the day, all through 365 days, with the click of a button.

But, we are fools, and for fear of losing the good fortune, immediately sent it to as many friends as possible, and came back, and went to bed peacefully, dreaming of the riches that the Nagapushpa would bring in immediately. Over and above that, in doing so,(sharing this wonderful secret of god), fulfilling our part of ***Loka samastha sukhino bhavanthtu*** (Let all the people in the world be happy. Let all the world be happy.).See, we Indians are very religious and well versed in the puranas,so that we always do good things!!!. And we Keralites have the greatest literacy including internet usage among all Indians, and hence, probably, we shared it to the maximum.

Being a fool is blissful.

Fools of the world, if you have any chance, put this fool's own country to be the first place to visit in your lifetime.

CHAPTER X

The case of the unpaid dues

In one of the villages in Kerala, there was a large contractor who runs almost every business in the village. Over the years, this man became the sole person responsible for every development of the place and was the decision maker in almost all the things in the hamlet. Things were going on well, when once, a large forest fire broke out in the village. Many people were killed, and many lost their property, and means of livelihood. Overnight, people became refugees, with nothing to claim as their own. That was traumatic for the whole lot and many were on the verge of mental breakdown, and not able to cope up with the harsh reality that they are penniless and hapless. There were lots of people, who were unaffected, and during the initial days of the calamity, all people joined hands, forgetting differences over caste, creed, gender, former quarrels and the like, and it was just a wonderful example of great camaraderie and brotherhood for the whole world. People from around the world praised the oneness of the land.Crew from the world's best TV sites came to the state to tell the story of the devastation and the helping hands of the people in times of distress. Actually, people from far and wide, from all nooks of the state and from all walks of life, came to the village for rescue and relief operations. Relief materials flowed to the relief camps in all forms, like food, clothing, sanitation items and all things needed to clean the debris of what was left after the fire. Money for relief flowed in from helping minds in tens and thousands. This was kept as separae account, and since the contractor was the only accepatable self in the hamlet, he was kept as the custodian and manager of the funds. This was to be named as the relief fund. From this fund, the contractor was to distribute to the needy, based on their requirements and the loss they incurred.

It was also decided that everybody working under various divisions in his company would contribute generously, but voluntarily to the relief and disaster management fund. There was one division under him, which looked into power generation for the various projects. As was usual with all divisions, this unit also had a separate income and expenditure audit and all such things. It was also necessary for the unit to seek expertise from other companies outside the village, and give consultation fee etc. for them. Due to the fire, this unit had to reconstruct the whole infrastructure, and there was heavy cash crunch. They were running the show by borrowing money from their bankers, at about 3% more interest than the prevailing rates, a facility known as overdraft. That is, they have no money in their accounts, but the bank is giving credit at this very high rate, ignoring the inherent risk that they are giving this loan to a penniless firm. The contractor-manager had a lot of money as dues to this power unit, which was the cost of power consumed by his other units. The dues came to about 800 lakhs. Even in this condition, when the contractor was to pay this small power unit, a hefty sum of 800 lakhs, they had to take the overdraft at normal plus three percent interest to pay salary to their workers.

After the fire ended, the workers in the power unit, as also workers from other similar units under the contractor decided to contribute a small sum from their monthly wages towards the relief fund, to be paid every month for one full year, to facilitate the rebuilding process. This amount, collected by the power unit, month after month, was earmarked as a separate fund and kept in a separate account, but was not transferred to the relief fund every month. The total contribution towards this was less than one lakh per month, and the total per year came to less than 12 lakhs.

The amount of money that was obtained as relief fund, being operated by the contractor came to many million. It was also found that only a fraction of the money in the relief fund under this very same contractor had been spent towards relief and rehabilitation and a large sum was lying with the contractor, unused, and accruing no interest. *(If you are not aware of it, any money that does not earn interest is making you poorer by the day, because,in an inflationary economy like that of India, what you get after a few years is money that has lesser purchasing power due to inflation. So, actually you are losing money.)* In a normal situation, anybody in their senses would have adjusted this small contribution from the workers of the power unit, totalling to about one lakh per month, towards the amount of around 800 lakhs which was the dues owed by the contractor to the power unit and accordingly made adjustments in the book. This power unit did not even do this, but at the end of the year, decided to remit the contribution money accrued for the whole year, totalling to about 12 lakhs to the fund as one time payment. They were again requesting that the huge dues to them may be paid immediately, since they were borrowing money at 3% extra rates for paying salary and also for buying things for the rebuilding of power lines and other infrastructure.

Now is the time when the great malayalees with his inborn talent for quarrel and argument came to the fore. This came as an audit objection from the auditors. Their objection was like this

"Why did the power unit keep the money with them all the year? Why they did not transfer this every month to the relief fund?

"But sir, they owe us around 800 lakhs, and this is just about one lakh per month. They are not giving us our dues."

If you have dues to be obtained, continue to ask for it, put a reminder if it does not come, if still nothing comes, continue to put reminders. That is part of the fiscal management that every expert has to do". This is how the argument continues.

It is as though the power unit had done some great sin, keeping about 12 lakhs with them, while they were to get 800 lakhs as dues. Funny?Right?

I heard a rumour that a similar situation happened in the case of the Kerala state Electricity Board (KSEB) and the Kerala disaster fund. But I am making my situation very clear. I have no knowledge about even the existence of such a row, that is currently being blown up as a great sin by our own media, both print and visual. I am deaf , dumb and blind when you talk about that.

But the contractor story that I explained tells us why we are called a fools' own country. Nobody thinks in the right way. If you put some correct argument, they will never buy it. But if you put the most foolish one, they will swallow it even without a pinch of salt. That is what we are.

And we proudly proclaim ourselves as Fools' own country.

CHAPTER XI

Hartal's own country

Until recently, there was another ritualistic custom that we Keralites observed religiously. This was called as hartal. This word has a Hindi origin, meaning ***hat thala*** or put a lock to the shop. This was generally used in olden times to close down the shops in protest against some action of the government and to seek their intervention to solve the issue. A still intense form of this protest is called as Bandh, meaning closure. This would affect everything, including public transport, shops, industry and every establishment. This was supposedly a very extreme step, and was used only in the rarest of rare occasions in the country. The reason being that, it also had, in itself, an element of self-destruction. Everybody suffered and unless such a suffering is vindicated, this measure of protest was never resorted to.

But we Keralites are different. We have a tradition of electing the world's first communist government, and protests are a way of life to us. So, if Iraq invades Kuwait or Iraq invades Iran or vice versa, or , for that matter, any international event, there are people who would form a procession or jatha as we call it, and shout slogans aloud, walk through streets, make a gathering, make some public speeches, spent around a few hours, rejoicing in this waste of time, and go back peacefully to their house , contended that we have done our duty of doing a protest. If you ask one of them, why this protest and what is the ultimate outcome of the protest, and whether it was not a waste of your time, the answer of the typical Keralite is that "you have to **react** to any and all injustice". Even when we point out that nobody, even in the next state will come to know of your protest, let alone Iran or Iraq, the response is the same.

We have to protest against injustice. That is what a civilized free thinking person has to do.That is a social responsibility that every civilized person has to do. Otherwise what is the difference between you, the educated man, and illiterates?

So, such things continued unabatedly and the number of people joining such "jathas"were on the rise through the years. In this, we literally followed the Bhagavat Gita, in which it is written "***Karmanye Vadhikaraste, Ma phaleshou kada chana*** – You have a right to perform your prescribed duty, but you are not entitled to the fruits of actions. ... In simple terms it means:

Keep on performing your duties without expecting any reward in return, leading a selfless life – this it what it is all about".

So friends, we are an elitist society working for this.

Even for the atheist, this was true, but they had some other manifesto or other book which supported exactly this action of theirs. So, as I was saying, we are a society of reactionaries, and hence it is important for us to call a bandh for every perceivable reason.

We were the persons who called a bandh, when Saddam Hussein was hanged by the US forces.

We also observed bandh, when Bill Clinton came to Bangalore, because he was *persona non grata* for us. He was having a past in which he had supposedly extravagant sexual deeds with his secretary or the like. None of the bangaloreans felt bad about his visit, and the official machinery of Karnataka, responsible for his tour did their duty, and Clinton went back, without ever even knowing that the next state Kerala was at a standstill for the whole day due to him.

At least a dozen bandhs were to protest against the fuel price hike by the central government/the petroleum companies. Not even once, even a single paisa was reduced due to this.

In some cases, the national bandh was called for by the National political parties, but most states, people simply went along with their jobs, and it was never felt anywhere. But , in Kerala, the slightest provocation causes a healthy bandh.

As the years passed, some relaxation came to the serene observance of the bandh, and instead of the 24 hour bandh, it was reduced to a 6AM-6PM event. This was of very practical significance. We Keralites, as you all know, have certain habits, glued to our DNA. The morning newspaper is one. Everybody reads the morning newspaper along with his bed tea, and without that, the day cannot start. Many others do the reading in the toilet, and the defecation is not complete without the paper. On days like August 16th , (The day after independence day , when, because the previous day was a national holiday, there will be no newspaper for that day), October 3rd (next to Gandhi Jayanthi) and other national holidays, these people will read the previous day's paper again, this time more intently, covering whatever news was unknowingly let off the previous day. In so doing, they fulfill their routine and finish off their chores.

So, if on a bandh day, you cannot read the newspaper, which is delivered in the wee hours, life comes to a standstill. So newspapers were left out from the ambit of Hartal. Also, milk packets (Due to the obvious reason that you cannot miss your morning tea) and hospitals were also left out from the hartal and bandh. One more practical difficulty was there. Even though you could place road blockades with big stones and tree logs etc., late in the night, this could be done only on a limited scale. And the pro hartal people could be mobilized only a few hours after daybreak. So, we are also practical minded, so that the bandh got itself converted to 6AM to 6PM. Some nasty fools were always there, who would try to run the public transport buses, but they were rightfully handled by throwing stones, and destroying the bus, so that they would never venture out again in their life. Shops that were opened were systematically attacked, and the bandh would be made successful.

I was also thinking, why, at the slightest provocation, the shop owners were downing their shutters. A record total of 223 harthals were observed in 2006, resulting in a revenue loss of over ?2000 crore. There were around 363 of "Hartals", called by different political parties, between 2005 and 2012. As I said earlier, Hartals are called for various reasons, political, economic and social. Annoyed by the revenue loss to the exchequer, loss of livelihood to daily wage earners, and inconvenience caused to the general public at large, the full bench of the Kerala high court banned bandhs in 1997. The then Left government filed a petition to get the order reversed, but was shot down by the supreme court of India.

However, you cannot beat the Keralite, who is hell bent on self destruction. We promptly renamed what was practically a bandh call, into a call for a 'hartal' to get around the law. reacting to this new form of bandh in a new name, in the year 2000, the Kerala high court ruled that the enforcement of a hartal by **"force, intimidation – physical or mental – and coercion"** was unconstitutional. This, however, did not discourage Kerala's politicians and others who wanted to celebrate Hartals. Indian National Trade Union Confederation (INTUC) Kerala vice president an ex-parliamentarian, at some time clarified that hartals are not the same as workers' strikes. So, many hartals were called as transport workers strike, shop owners strike, and various other strikes. Obviously, none of these were based on 100 percent acceptance by the concerned unions, but a miniscule fraction of them. "Workers' strike cannot be seen like Hartals . They are forced to strike for their survival."

Signs of improvement

According to a document from the State Planning Board, 85,000 person-days were lost due to strikes in Kerala in the financial year 2017 (up to July), as against 2.68 lakh in the year up to July 2013. It was revealed that informal workers were hit hardestin any hartal. The tourism sector, a mainstay of the Kerala economy, was bleeding from the impact of frequent hartals. Some 50,000 domestic and foreign tourists were trapped indoors due to the state-wide shutdown during one year. In Kochi, "Around 2,500 foreign tourists – mostly from the UK and Germany – who arrived by a chartered flight and four cruise ships were left in the lurch when Kochi shut down."In the informal sector workers are hurt most. In general, wages in the formal economy are not cut due to hartal absences; firms often ask for work on weekends or extended working hours to make up for the lost time. Informal workers are forced to stay at home, and lose their day's income.

"People like us, who depend on daily business, who do business on the streets, are the ones who are the most affected," one street vendor said.

"I need Rs 1,000 every day for survival. My parents need medicines worth Rs 600 daily. With the remaining Rs 400, my family survives. It's stressful and painful when we lose even one day's business."

The situation continued for many more years. Then, on one occasion, fed up with the loss of working days and the damage hartal's do to public life, the Kerala high court summoned one prominent youth leader of a political party and asked him to explain why he should not be ordered to pay damages in a hartal proclaimed by him and his followers.

The leader escaped by saying some excuses, but the court issued strict warnings. Thence forth, even if there are political killings, lathi charges or other police atrocities and other compelling reasons, the hartals are not declared for the whole state, but are confined to the small localities around the scene. These usually do not attract the wrath of the court and we are happy to be free of hartals now.

Hartals...we miss you dearly.

Regards- Your dear Fools' own country

CHAPTER XII

Nottirattippikkal or "double your money with us"

In Malayalam, this word Nottirattippikkal means doubling of currency notes. This is another form of cheating that has been tried from very early times, and has also come in the newspapers, many times every year. But the Keralite with his great wisdom refuses to learn, and every year, this type of fraud is done very frequently. Some are known, but the majority is not even booked, because those who were cheated are too ashamed as well as incapable to complain, because what they tried to do was unlawful.

There are many variations in this type of cheating, but essentially, this is to exploit the greed of human beings for making a lot of money even unlawfully.

Let us take one example.

If you are known to be greedy for money, you will be spotted. Somehow, these fraudsters will locate the gullible people. The first intimation to the poor fool is that they have a mechanism by which they will double your money. However, as is mutually agreed, nobody should know this, because it is illegitimate. To make you understand why this is done, they will make you believe that they have a lot of black money that is to be converted to legitimate white money. They will give you double the money that you are giving, if you can give them a cash cheque. So, they will get a cheque for your bank account and will give you twice the amount. Bundles of notes for twice the money is handed over to you. Someway they will fool you into agreeing that you will not count the money that has been given, until they claim their cheque and leave the place. They will encash it and vanish, but when the bundle of notes that they gave are verified, then only the fooling is detected. What they have given you would be just bundles of paper cut in the size of notes with currency only at the top and bottom of each bundle. So, what you get are a few notes of the denomination, plus neatly cut paper pieces. You can use them for the rest of your whole life for writing your everyday shopping list, so that you remember what a great fool you were.

Another method is to tell you that what they are offering are counterfeit notes, but which is as good as original, and you will never be caught. To make you believe that the notes offered are so perfect like the original, they will ask you to pay some money and give counterfeits for double that money. With that, they will shop in the hotels and shops taking you also with them to prove the genuineness of their claim and will come out unscathed. Then they will ask you to do the shopping with the notes they gave you. Then also, nobody will object, and you are convinced.

Now that you have made sure that their counterfeit is more genuine than the original, you will, in your greed, give lakhs of rupees as much as your greed demands. You might even sell your gold to pay for this illicit transaction, because, you can buy double the quantity the very next day. You are happy and in the shade of darkness or dim light, you are given bundles of money (Counterfeit, but more genuine than the RBI notes, as you have verified) for double the denomination that you have given. But, if you try to transact business with those counterfeit notes, you will be caught sooner than your expectation. This is one situation.

In another type of conning, you may be given bundles having genuine notes only on top and bottom and with just paper cut in the size in between. This, you are lucky, because you won't be caught by the police, but would just swallow the ignominy and suffer mutely. Now, if you are wondering how the counterfeit notes were accepted in all the trial runs, there is a bitter truth. Those were real genuine notes printed by RBI and were never counterfeit. You were made to believe that they were counterfeit, but how can you be caught for dealing in genuine currency. You get fooled only in the second part of the drama. Many similar tricks are ingeniously developed and implemented, successfully every year. The great fools of this small fully literate state, queue up to be made fools every time.

I love you, my brethren, for being such wonderful fools.

Welcome, fools' own country

CHAPTER XIII

Bio composting with pipe composting

As I mentioned earlier, we are the first to accept any new technology. We are also probably the worlds' greatest hypocrites, to profess one in public and to act entirely to the contrary when it comes to our own personal affairs. So, we have a great number of NGOs and activist groups that strive to protect the environment day in and day out. In the last few years, and still is, waste management was one of the prime concerns of all panchayats, and other local bodies. People of all societal gradation were throwing their domestic waste in isolated places in the city and even small towns. This included kitchen waste, left over food, garbage, waste from slaughter houses and everything waste.

The problem was that all these were tied in plastic bags and thrown on the sides of roads or in deserted lands. The situation was very bad, because in their haste to dispose of this stinking stuff without being caught, in many instances, the waste gets thrown in the road itself. Later this gets run over by vehicles, and makes a stinking mess for days together. There were no exceptions to this behavior from every person in every walk of life. Many would proclaim eco-friendly behavior and the need to compost these waste and to manage it in an ecofriendly way, but when it comes to their own waste, they will all do the very same.

So, the local self-government bodies found out a new method of composting food waste and left over vegetable cuttings etc. using cement pipes or plastic pipes. Two pipes of 25 cm diameter and 150 cm height were given free to most households. These were dug into the soil for a small depth and waste was to be put inside one of the pipes. When one pipe gets filled, the second one was to be used. Theoretically, waste in the first pipe will get decomposed fast, and by the time the second gets filled, the waste in the first pipe gets fully digested. At that time, you can remove the well digested compost, and use it for your plants and crops., adding to the fertility of the soil. The next one will then start decomposing and you can use the one from which you have removed the compost for filling waste afresh.

That was a wonderful pipe dream.

In practice, different households had different quantities of waste and would not cater to their needs in most cases. That was pardonable, but during rains, the water also got inside and caused the semi decayed mess from the pipes to start seeping out, giving wonderful aroma all around and inside the house making life miserable. Added to this was the nuisance from rats, scavenger birds and all other related animal and plant population. Even though the programme was launched with much fanfare, involving public meetings for distribution of the pipes by local polititians and the like, and conducted with much fanfare, but ultimately, it ended up in wasting public money for such foolish acts.

All fools around, would sanction the project and gather to attend the inauguration meetings and distribution functions. The event will be covered in the local press, local TV and also social media. We will see the faces of these great dignitaries presenting the pipes to the beneficiaries, and all of them grinning quixotically.In a matter of a few weeks to a few months, these pipes were abandoned, and were dumped in the backyards, or better still, disposed off to junk dealers. Needless to say, all fools clapped initially for this foolish decision. If anyone had objected to this waste spending and tried to explain the technological flaws in this venture, he or she would have been punished by stone throwing either in person or by social media ostracizing or some such stringent retaliatory measures. Wise people will keep their mouths shut, and we, in the fool's own country, will be forced to make a celebration of it.

Fools of the world, you are welcome.

CHAPTER XIV

STP- Sewage treatment plants in high rise buildings.

What were we doing in olden years to treat the human excreta in the household? Long years back, it was open defaecation in the wilderness, and still later, it was physically removed by the lowly paid unfortunate souls. At least in parts of North India, it is heard that the practice of humans aiding in scavenging every day is still in vogue. Most unfortunate, right?

But in Kerala, as far as my memory dates back, most people had toilets in their dwellings. These toilets were equipped with a septic tank, and the excreta would be processed by the naturally occurring bacteria over a period of time. It would be almost fully digested, and may be, once in ten years or so, the accumulated slurry would be removed. This was done by humans in the earlier times, but now, there are specialists doing this with motorized pumps and containers to collect it and dispose it off in far off isolated places where it gets digested and is actually a good organic matter.

Except for the stigma associated with it, compost and the slurry from human excreta would in no way be different from those made from cows or other cattle or other animals in their capacity to enrich the soil and fertilise it. This was going on peacefully, until some very wise town planner diagnosed that with lots and lots of multistoried flats boomeranging in all metros and even small towns, the old septic tank system cannot solve the problems of excreta decomposition.

In our country, most of the reforms that are made to rectify an apparently faulty system is to replace it with a costlier and complicated system that would in no way solve the problem, but would make it more complex. It would necessitate various protocols and procedures, so that there is scope for interpreting it in unimaginably diverse ways. This would allow the implementing agencies to classify the rules in various ways to put incurable obstacles into the implementation of the system. All this, as you should know, is to make room for forcing the poor taxpayer on the other end of the counter to offer bribe to get out of the imbroglio.

So, in the current context, the system of septic tank was dispensed with. Newly constructed multi storied flats were ordered by law to change from septic tanks to modern sewage treatment plants or STP in short. The waste water and slurry should be treated, and made into sludge, water and gas only. There would be absolutely no waste and the treated water that comes out of the STP should be so pure that it can be even used for drinking.

What an idea serjee!

But in practice, I have personally known that the system is very faulty, and very costly to maintain. However, since it is the law, everybody is forced to obey. If you ask any flat owner about STP, the first thing that they will complain is the very bad smell of Hydrogen sulfide that they are forced to suffer. Along with this, there are other foul smelling gases and methane also emitting out. Whatever be the solution, like adding bacteria and various other ways, it will never be a substitute for the "fit and forget" septic tanks that we had earlier.

Now, I will try to make you familiar with the system. This involves initially, the stirring of the waste, then aerating it, allowing it to sediment; add chemicals for the settlement of the waste into water and sludge, and various pumps to operate all this. Ultimately, the supposedly divine water that comes out of the system has again to be pumped out. To my knowledge, there are at least six or seven pumps that are necessary in all these operations. Needless to say, they all add up drastically to the power consumption. There is also the requirement of everyday servicing of the system to add chemicals to the STP plant. There should also be some person to operate the pumps of the plant every day for different durations and at specified intervals. Even with all these, the outcome is that when the pump is switched on, the unbearable foul smell spreads in the whole area. So the remedy has become more problematic than the problem itself. And if by sheer bad luck, one of the pumps fails, you have to lift it from the sludge, because all of them are submersible pumps, or, in other words, they are deep down inside the waste pool. And, it has to be repaired on a war footing, or otherwise, nobody in the flat system can go to the toilets or even urinate. Add to this, the perpetual complaint and animosity from the neighbours around the flats for disrupting their surroundings with foul smelling gas.

I was unfortunate to be either the secretary or President of an eleven storied apartment complex for a few years and had firsthand experience with this complicated system. There is also a pollution control board that has to give a certificate to the flats that their STP is working well according to mandatory stipulations. Not to be outdone, they also specify some unwanted modification every year. The flats have to pay 75000 rupees every three years as fees to the pollution control board. I once had an occasion to visit the office of the pollution control board in Thrissur. And, true to its short name as pollution board, the whole area was polluted and littered with garbage, domestic waste and what not. I don't know what the situation is now.

And, interestingly, what the PCB wants to implement every year is a modification of the existing syetem to get rid of all these smell and other problems. After implementing a system that was supposed to solve all problems of sewage,we have to continually improve the system. This is by modifying the old one which was the panacea of yester years. Again, you have to spend money for refurbishing, but the maintenance also becomes more costly. All this, when we had a fit and forget system that was time tested.

However, this wonderfully foolish system of self-perpetuating pollution development system that is affectionately called as the Sewage Treatment Plant, is not confined to Kerala and is a national disaster. The reason for these that comes to my mind is that once you have elected your government for ruling you, you have to suffer until their term is over. And, over the years, it is our experience that governments cannot survive without putting stumbling blocks into the everyday life of every common man. Our humble day dream is that there has to be a no fuss, human intervention free, self-contained, ecofriendly method of waste destruction just as in the case of the bio digester toilets that the Indian Railways have introduced. Remember, before the introduction of this intervention, the Indian railways were the longest public defaecation system in the whole of the world. Those days, railway stations were stinking with the smell of human excreta accumulated in between the rails.

So now, we are the leading population in the implementation of this foolish disastrous interference that is called as STP. We , in Kerala, are proud as being the pioneering fools for the whole country, but are also satisfied that the whole country is slowly joining the bandwagon of the most literate fools.

Let the example of our state as being fools' own country be the leading spirit for the whole country.

CHAPTER XV

Pepsi and Coca cola are toxic.

This is another great finding that took Kerala by storm. It should be confessed, that it was propagated by illiterate fools and also by politically inclined souls who gulp down doctrines and explanations given by their leaders to anything and everything under the sun. In many instances, I have personally been pained to observe first hand, the subservience of people with even Ph.D. and or otherwise very well educated men and women gulping down these blatant mistakes and misgivings, without even the slightest amount of protest or scientific thinking. In the case of those who follow political parties, be they left, centre or right, it makes us wonder how people can believe such foolish arguments, which even a school student would question. In another case, it is the so called playwrights, novelists or other literary luminaries who blindly proclaim many half-truths as legitimate information and vehemently argue for it.

The case of Endosulfan induced illnesses in Kerala is a case in point. But, with the advent of social media and ease of making things in a make believe fashion, and editing things to suit a particular goal, it is very difficult for us to differentiate between chaff and grain in any media content. I would say the greatest fools on earth are those, who, even without fully reading the content, immediately share it. This is based on a psychology to proclaim to the world, (or at least the limited circle of friends that he or she has access to,) that I knew all these things ages before, and is an authority or well knowledgeable in all these complex things or subjects in the world. Unfortunately, by doing so, and sharing half-baked truths or (in most instances, utter nonsense!) these people expose themselves as despicable fools. But even close friends will not reveal these to such people in order to keep the friendship going and not to irk the poor soul's ego.

Let me cite an example of a heated propaganda against synthetic drinks like Coca cola and Pepsi in the last decade. The original media unleashed animosity against a particular company was that of a Coca cola factory that was established in Plachimada, a non-descript village in Palakkad district of Kerala. It is captioned as The Plachimada Coca-Cola Struggle and "was a series of protests to close the Coca-Cola factory in the village of Plachimada, Palakkad District, Kerala in the early 2000s". Villagers noted that soon after the factory opened, their wells started to run dry and the available water turned contaminated and toxic. Soon, waste from the factory was passed off to farmers in the area as fertiliser. The factory employed 130 permanent workers and approximately 250 temporary laborers. Brands produced at the Plachimada factory included Coca-Cola, Limca, Fanta, Thums Up, Sprite, Kinley Soda, and Maaza.

On 22 April 2002, the villagers, mostly Adivasi(tribals), began to protest in front of the factory by blocking its entrance. The impromptu protest continued and lasted for years, by gathering support from environmental groups, locals and national political parties and activists. Continued protests and litigation eventually helped the people of Plachimada to shut down the factory in March 2004". One thing that has to be noted here is that while the 32 acre Plachimada plant is on the side of the Chittur –meenakshipuram highway, I am not in a position to clearly demarcate the tribal settlements from which these people came for the protests. We also have to be aware of a report in the press in 2019 that says that Fifteen years after a people's agitation shut down a Coca Cola bottling plant, the water table is yet to recover." If you read it the other way round, and think logically, you will have to accept that the so called water exploitation by the company was just one of the excuses to force the company to shut down.

Otherwise, the water table should have recovered to its original level in the next fifteen years of rainfall.

This is how the very same things that you express in the newspapers can be useful in finding the truth, if you are not a blind follower alone, of the text that you read.

"The factory had also made a practice of distributing its sludge waste from the manufacturing process as free fertilizer to the villagers. In 2003, a BBC journalist visited the village to investigate the claims made by the villagers that the sludge was contaminated. As part of his reporting for BBC Radio 4's **Face the Facts,** he had picked up samples of the sludge and sent to the United Kingdom to be analyzed. A lab at the University of Exeter found unacceptably high levels of cadmium and lead in the sludge. Interestingly, there are no reports that any of the labs in any part of the country had made such an analysis and published a report. What comes to my mind is a recent post in social media that a rubber plant in one of the estates produced a jack fruit in its trunk. There was also a photo of it.

The person who made that post had a clear intention to make the readers aware that it was just a fun. He gave a <u>PDF in the guise of a press report</u>

with no identity of the newspaper, as a press cutting. The photo, was clearly a Photoshop product. The content was also so unauthentic with the name of the panchayat president to have made an unnatural statement. However, the place in reference was a municipality. To make things more explicit, he also gave an 11-digit contact number, which, as all of us fools know, does not exist in India. He also claimed that scientists from Agricultural university visited the site and took samples that they sent to All in One university of Saudi Arabia. All These were fictitious, because he never said the Kerala Agri university was involved. There is no All in One university, and to send it to Saudi Arabia, where there is not even (may be) jack Tree. **The sad part, I should confess, is that it was informed that at least some professors from the local Agricultural University shared the information.** How pitiful, deplorable, and worthless. It is such people from all walks of life including the press, that make a mountain of a mole hill. *My respectful homage to those souls, because they would be more at home in the nether world than in this living earth.*

Actually, grapevine says that Coca cola being a multinational, the local political leaders asked for a hefty sum as bribe or commission for allowing the company to work peacefully. Rumour says that the company agreed for half the amount or so, but that it was not acceptable to the other side. So, it was decided by these people that the plant will not be allowed to function properly. I would say that the print and visual media, without even a single exception, played an active role in fomenting and propagating unverified facts as truths. First, it was that the factory was producing toxic sludge with contaminants like cadmium and lead and other heavy metals. They also gave examples of sufferers in other countries like the Mina Mata episode in japan,(Mina Mata disease was first discovered in the city of Minamata, Kumamoto Prefecture, Japan, in 1956, hence its name. It was caused by the release of methyl mercury in the industrial wastewater from a chemical factory owned by the Chisso Corporation, which continued from 1932 to 1968). Similar havoc stories from Karnataka and other places were also described to make people concerned that this sort of things have happened in India also in the past and that we should be vigilant to prevent such things from happening again in Kerala.

And, in this "struggle for livelihood of the down trodden and penniless, and for conservation of the Ecosystem," an NGO from Delhi also played a vital role. They published a survey that showed lot of toxic residues in many of coco cola and Pepsi products. Out of curiosity,I verified the data published by them. It must still be available in print. They had given the toxicity levels in many products by these factories in ppm and ppb (Parts per million or parts per billion) etc. Unfortunately, the number of samples that they analysed in each brand was two, there or even in one case, just one sample from a single bottle. Mind you, the total production from each of these factories runs to at least one lakh bottles of each brand per day. And to analyse just one from them and publish the results as authentic validation of contaminants from the factory? Where are statistical procedures, verification and validation?? It is just like taking a single sand particle from an acre of seashore and if it had traces of gold, to decare the whole plot as golden beach. Anybody with the least exposure to science would have burnt it as trash, the moment it was produced. The Coca cola bottling plant at Palakkad was closed down due to this and many other reasons.

The only thing that we gained was shutting down the plant and leaving thousands jobless. There is also another paradox in this case because, just kilometres away, in Kanjikode, the Pepsi Company was operating years before the Coca cola plant, and continued production in all the years of the agitation until in 2020, when they decided to close down on their own.They had other reasons to close it down. The cola company actually dismantled their plant and relocated it in some other state. They still supply Cola and Pepsi in the whole of Kerala and new gen youngsters drink this without any inhibition. Now my question is, if you want to eliminate Cola due to its contaminants from the factory and depletion of groundwater, why do you allow the same products inside Kerala now a days and drink it, and make the people near those factories outside Kerala to suffer the very same bad effects?

To speak the truth,it is only lack of worldly exposure that made us fools in Kerala to silently watch all these agitations without even a single line of protest. All because, if you expose the ignorance and protest, you will be branded as a capitalist stooge, multinational paid traitor and what not. Anybody who had made an international travel to Europe would always know that once you are in their skies, they don't normally serve you chai as we call tea, but just coke. In many flights, tea is not even available. Don't think that as is in vogue in Kerala, "one tea, without, one medium tea and two double strong with less sugar etc." are not common in other parts of the world. These are phrases to be heard only in local teashops and is not an international beverage request. The world over they still gulp down millions of gallons of both Pepsi and Cola every day.

Another funny thing is to show videos where Coke and Cola are used to kill worms, cockroaches etc. The truth is that if you put them in carbonated sugar or salt water or soap water also, they will die.

Any way, we survive by being fools.

Three cheers to my Fools' own country

CHAPTER XVI

Paracetamol is toxic

When it comes to propagating the most unthinkable and unreasonable foolishness,I will rate my own brethren in the state of Kerala as the world number one. Here is an example, where it was widely propagated some time back that even the common anti fever drug Paracetamol is toxic. Now a day, with covid looming large in the lives of everybody in every conceivable way, Paracetamol is one of the most popular medicines consumed by almost every person.

But a few years back, there was a lot of propaganda in the public platforms that **Paracetamol was toxic** to humans and produced very severe health problems and that it can even cause death. But this did not gain much leverage, not because that many educated people made serious literature search into it, (*and found that there was no substance to it,*) but solely because there was no substitute drug comparable in price and as equally effective enough to replace Paracetamol. Even this year, in a little read news platform, I had the chance to read again that Dolo 650(the same Paracetamol) is toxic and that it can cause health problems. Again, even those who might have read it took it seriously because we cannot afford to have any other medicine to fight the covid or fever.

It was neccessary for me to search the original article to find out the truth behind it.

I havc a inding from onc of the articles reproduced below.

Paracetamol in high single doses (typically 15 g or more) causes liver injury through a toxic metabolite, NAPQI (N-acetyl-p-benzoquinone imine). Alcohol consumption and possibly starvation induce cytocrome P-450 and therefore increase NAPQI synthesis. These factors also contribute to glutathione depletion, [23, 24] thus enhancing paracetamol hepatotoxicity. Therefore, heavy drinkers would be at high risk of liver toxicity with paracetamol taken in relatively high doses.

In the case of the original mention in the media that I remember, may be a decade back, even a reference to the original research that found Paracetamol as toxic, was given. Almost nobody verified the claims. But due to sheer curiosity, I read the article again. I dont remember the exact dose or so, but it said something like this --- if you are taking 60 gm of Paracetamol continuously for 15 days or so, there is likelihood that you will lose your kidneys, will have problems for heart, or other organs etc. It doesn't specify whether it was done on other mammals or an estimate, but, even if it were true, just analyse it. The normal Paracetamol that we take is only 500 mg, thrice or 4 times a day, so the total is around 4 gm per day. Even if you take it for a week, the total that you consume is just 14 gm. Compare this with about 60 gm per day. That means, 120 tablets per day. Are you serious, 120 tablets? How deceitful???We never go into the fine print and start propagating the foolishness. In other words, are you talking about breakfast, lunch and supper"? Quixotic, right?

However, the report that I have put up above which states 15 gms in single dose is one that has appeared in scientific journals and is available in the internet. But here also, you should consider that the toxic dose to cause liver damage is 15 gms, or otherwise, 30 tablets.

We should understand that these researches are all done to safeguard humanity about the safety drugs, and in no case should be reported out of context. Experts have their own standards and taking anything out of context is always the most foolsih thing. Don't ever do it.

But still, a lot of us genetically programmed and internationally acclaimed fools in this part of the country gleefully shared this information for aiding the general health of all our brethren in this state and elsewhere in the world. I am proud of my state's accredited fools for their great humanitarian feelings.

Welcome to fools own country.

CHAPTER XVII

Broiler reared chicken is contaminated-they use antibiotics and tender coconut is full of insecticides

Poultry rearing is a profitable business, but needs careful rearing standards to make it profitable. Otherwise, they are prone to diseases and many other things that wipe of the entire colony. Sometimes it happens that some disease is reported for chicken in some parts of the our state or neighbouring Tamil Nadu. Most of our chicken comes from Tamil Nadu. There are only very few poultry farms in the state. The reason is obvious. You cannot cope with the wage structure in Kerala and produce chicken in an economical way. Add to this, the trade unionism, donations to local, district and state units of all political parties, temples, mosques and churches, social organisations, goons and what not. So, even if you start such a bold venture, you will have to close shop in no time.

So, in reality, the bulk producer is Namakkal, a village in Tamil Nadu. Production runs into millions and is probably the biggest distribution centre in that state. What happens is that during some periods, birds get affected by some pandemic and they are forced to destroy the whole stock. Immediately, the price will get hiked up due to shortage of birds, but demand also would fall, because of the fear of diseased birds being sold. Later, when fresh batches arrive after a few weeks, prices will naturally go down. In between these happenings, a certain set of anti-social minded gossip mongers will start publishing information that the chicken from these vendors are given very heavy doses of antibiotic as matter of routine, and in very high doses that are harmful to human beings. The most picked up scaring point is that if you are consuming these chicken, then you are prone to cancer. There are other ailments mentioned like heart attack, kidney trouble etc.., but the most favoured disease that these fellows warn you about is of course, cancer. There will naturally be a cautious approach to buying chicken for some time. The intention of these people are also just that.

But there are two things about we malayalees. The moment misinformation is shared, we make sure that on our part, we share it to the maximum and also discuss it threadbare in all social groups, be it in the bus, train, marriages, church gatherings, and every other place where just two or may be more people start a conversation. **The second thing is that, we cannot avoid eating chicken or meat in our everyday life.** So, in a few days, we forget what we publicized, and start eating these things again. Here, we follow something like what Mark twain is said to have remarked. *"It is very easy to quit smoking. I have done it a thousand times.* Similarly, we Keralites quit eating chicken very easily. We do the quitting a thousand times. Anybody with some sense of reality would easily understand that at the doses and frequencies of the antibiotics as mentioned in the media, (those drugs being very costly that if it were to be used the way they describe), each kg of meat would cost at least 1000 Rs per kilo!

In working out the economics of poultry farming, the thumb rule for broiler chicken is that you have to sell your stock within five to six weeks. After that even though the weight might increase, the marginal price increase is not supportive to the increased cost of feeding. In this balancing act, if you add the cost of these drugs also, it is not like painting a doomsday picture in the comfort of your room with a laptop or mobile. It is hard work and risk, along with physical involvement. But we fools become gossip mongers at more occasions than we really visualize.

Toxic tender coconut

Now, another that would run against the farmers in Tamil nadu and neighbouring states is about the tender coconut. Again, most of the tender coconut that is sold in Kerala comes from Tamil Nadu, and in the northern districts, from Karnataka. Here also, there are videos showing systematic feeding of toxic pesticides through the roots and cautioning us about cancer and the like. The simple fact that life still continues in all the states of the country, despite the increased consumption of tender coconuts in the summer months, just means that there is something wrong with the video. My personal experience with this sort of root feeding is that the plant never absorbs these at these heavy concentrations because, the level of concentration in the plastic bag below the root is more than the cell sap concentration. So, according to science, what must happen is exosmosis, where, the cell sap would flow back into the polythene cover. But the plant knows better, and the root tip will get scorched, and will dry up eventually so that no chemical will get inside. Similar stories about excessive use of pesticides in vegetables and other crops are also publicized. I do accept that the usage is not within the acceptable or required levels, and much of it could be avoided by careful planning and integrated pest management. But, the way fear psychosis is created, we all would have been dead meat long long before. So, for us fools in this part of the country who propagate foolishness for some time, and conveniently forget it to choose our taste, let me give them a big salute.

*It is not for nothing that the adage has been created- **“Welcome to fools own country”.***

CHAPTER XVIII

The organic crop panacea or Everything Jaivam

Kerala is one state where the people tend to believe and accept whatever comes to them in print or electronic media, even though technically they are the most literate in the country. This is more so if anything is given as the opinion of a foreigner. More than 500 years of foreign rule has made us intellectual slaves, and we tend to overrate anybody outside the country as the authority, while our own experts are rated as below par, and not worthy of a serious consideration. As I mentioned earlier, if you see the number of forwards in whatsapp and the like that we receive everyday in social media and the number that we Keralites share and reshare, you will hit your head on the wall, saying oh, how many literate fools you have in your state?

Let me just take the example of organic farming and organic produce. Many of the ***so called*** experienced, elite farmers say that organic farming is the answer to all of our health problems. (I would add that most of these are celebrities, doing cultivation as a hobby, and has nothing to do with productivity of crops, their profitability or farming as a means of subsistence). Food that is branded as organic is supposed to solve all our health problems, including diabetes, low or high blood pressure, migraine, depression or, for that matter, anything that is considered as disease. This also includes major problems like heart attack and even cancer. The vegetables that we consume, mostly comes from outside the state, and is usually cultivated with fertilizers, and plant protection chemicals. Needless to say, they may also contain insecticides or other chemicals above the permissible levels. Strangely enough, there is a general tendency to link everything that is described as contaminated, to have a predisposing factor that ultimately leads to increased occurrence of cancer. No other disease other than cance has caught up with the imagination of our doomsday predictors and cautioning experts . And, strangely enough, none of these predictors (doing the indictment on specific products like ordinarily grown vegetables and other foods) explain which type of cancer these products will cause or have caused. It is easy to indict anything with cancer, and the readers do not even think for a fraction of a second to question which was the type of cancer ,where it has been reported, how many people were affected and the like.

It is just like seeking an alliance for your son or daughter. When you make enquiries, there are a good number of people who are hell bent on preventing good alliances. They give a lot of gossip as true facts, and the first thing that we do is to avoid the relationship. The argument is, why take a risk when there is an element of suspicion. You would never think that you may be the most affected if this was to happen to you and your child. But, generally, we tend to avoid risk and a caution is always done here. But again, we tend to forget that in the process, we have swallowed the most important thing that anybody with at least a little bit of brainpower would do first -finding out the facts.

Let us take the typical example with our daily foods. Mornings start with a cup of tea or coffee. And, the most well read knowledgeable person would get his organic tea or coffee in the morning, by paying a hefty price for the tea / coffee, that was displayed in the shop as organic. The great majority of others would simply gulp down the brew that is prepared from chai or coffee made from the dust brought from the local store. In more than 95 % of the situations, we don't have a choice to buy a product branded as organic or, we don't even know that there is a product available in the organic form. Neither is it possible to get such stuff in most of our villages, and towns. So now, let us analyse what this tea contains. Tea and coffee has a lot of pests, and are grown in large estates, or in a miniscule fraction, in small farms. **To say the truth, you cannot run a plantation profitably without using pesticides.**

(We have the tell tale example of the Sri Lankan tea industry which was on the verge of collapse due to the non use of chemical pesticides and fertilisers.)

But yes, some of these people set apart a small plot for organic, using minimal pesticides (but never fully stopping them) and sell it as organic product at a premium price. So, your tea has been sprayed with insecticides, but when it reaches you, in 99.9 percent of cases, they don't have any insecticides in the dangerous levels.

Now take your breakfast, which is basically from rice or wheat, and with curry or supplements from pulses or other sources. Invariably, the grain is from the nearby shop and is the item that you consume in the largest quantity. Unfortunately, it is almost impossible to get your requirement for the whole month entirely from an organic source. So, your food is never organic in its true sense. If you were accepting the argument that you will get cancer if you eat such foods, you would have died long long back. So, either the argument is wrong or you are a superhuman, resisting all sorts of pesticides in the contaminated food that you regularly eat. Congratulations, superman/woman. Let us also think of the pulses that you supplement in your breakfast. They are one of the items that are most prone to pests in the field and in the warehouse. Because of this, they are regularly sprayed in the storehouses. If this is not done, you will see that your arhar, cowpea, channa or greengram is full with beetle pests or their worms. This you must have noticed at least a few times in your life, where you forgot about the pulse that you purchased, and months later, when you spot it again, they are full with worms and beetles, right? This development of beetles and worms occur even in closed containers. So, the argument that your curry supplement for the breakfast is fully organic is again, wrong. But the funny thing about we malayalees or Keralites, is that we are very specific to proclaim that we eat organic food, without having even the mentality to cultivate our own organic food. And in the case of those who regularly post their organic produce like two brinjals, ten cowpeas, five ladies finger and the like, in facebook etc..never disclose how much is their daily requirement and how much of it comes from their own garden. Obviously, these are only exhibits, and not for regular consumption. Sure, you get a lot of likes and emojis, but , how many side dishes did you make out of it??

We regularly blame our farmer friends from the neighbouring states about over use of pesticides that they send to Kerala. The paradox or hard truth here is that without that, we can't even survive. Most of the grains, pulses, vegetables, fruits and even industrial goods come to Kerala from outside the state. We don't cultivate much of our lands, we don't have much of an industry and we don't even have sufficient workers. And to those fools who try to cultivate their lands, we, as political parties and their workers, will suffocate them out, so that they will never again try to do the misadventure. We are also the happiest lot to see that the industrialists are prevented from running successful ventures by organizing strikes almost regularly, and lockdowns and official interferences to block the smooth running of them. You would be pained if you can count the number of industries that have been permanently shut and kept rotting since Kerala came into existence as a state. Now, we don't toil in the fields, and that little area of land that we cultivate, is mostly done by people from outside the state, who are generally describe as Bengalis (even though they are also people from Rajastan, Madhya Pradesh, odisha and many other states. It is just like a North Indian calling anybody from south as Madrassi).Even most of the construction and other works that are taking place in the state, are done by these Bengalis.

However, we are most vociferous in supporting the newer things when they are launched. **Take the case of the one straw revolution that Fukuvoka, the Japanese farmer professed** .Decades back, it was much of a fashion to have seminars, and long discussions about the advantages of such practices and the damage that was being done to the health of people and the ecology by the normal cultivation that we followed. These meetings gave an opportunity for the *"easy chair farmers"* to eloquently speak about these practices, their advantages and the like, and get publicized in news media. Fortunately, almost none of the farmers were too educated to follow their words and nothing adverse happened. There are still many "Rip van winkles" in our state, who have not yet come out of the Fukuvoka hangover.

Most of us does not even know that when somebody sellsa produce as organic, you need an organic certification.

This is done by agencies that are licensed to do it, and they charge for it. It is a very expensive proposition to adhere to. Most of the agencies advice that you certify your most attractive, expensive produce as organic, and sell the others as normal food.

There is a second category that is certified as GAP, or following Good Agricultural Practices, which are cultivated on aneed based manner, with chemicals and fertilizers, but are always under supervision and strict adherence to norms. This also, is expensive to a certain extent.

There is a third category which is called as farmer certification, or participatory guarantee system or **PGS India.** This is decentralized organic farming certification system and is based on trust, and not really a verified organic system. But, as this system spreads more and more, farmers will compete for being truthful, and only the best will survive. However, as of today, most of the populace does not even know the existence of these rules and the officers concerned are not asking for an organic certificate from the vendors who display their produce as organic. So the cheating goes on. The slogan here, as one textile retailer giant put it as their bye line is **" Trust-is that not all"**

Well, it is just that –trust only. No guarantee. And we believe more in propaganda rather than truths.

As you know, we are fools' own country

CHAPTER XIX

Vyaja mutta(Duplicate egg) and plastic rice

Have you ever believed that you can manufacture an egg shell artificially, add some egg albumin inside with the yellow yolk in the middle, and then seal it with an air bubble inside? Still further, can you sell those eggs in the general market as genuine? If at all you succeed in making a single egg this way, will it not rot and produce an unbearably bad smell ? But with all these bare facts that you know exists, there are news reports about artificial eggs that are being systematically posted in even newspapers.

I am just copying below a series of links that eloquently laments about fake or duplicate eggs.

Beware Of Duplicate Eggs! 'Artificial Eggs' Return to Odisha ... https://www.youtube.com › watch 27-Jul-2020 —

Kanak News is Odisha's leading 24x7 news and current affairs TV channel from Eastern Media Limited. Odisha's largest media house that also ...

Latest News, Videos and Photos of fake eggs |

Times of India https://timesofindia.indiatimes.com › topic › fake-eggs

This is how you can distinguish between artificial and real eggs! https://zeenews.india.com › Health 01-Apr-2017 —

Cracking a real egg lightly will generate a crisp sound when compared to a fake egg.

And lastly, the fake eggs don't attract insects like ants ...

Fact Check: Plastic Eggs in Circulation in Indian Markets? https://thelogicalindian.com ›

Fact Check Claim: Fake eggs are being sold in the Indian markets. Claimed by: Social Media posts

Fact check by The Logical Indian: False Feedback Shocking! Fake eggs made of plastic being sold in markets of ..

. https://www.indiatoday.in › India › Video 31-Mar-2017 — Kolkata has been hit by a mass production of artificial eggs, allegedly made of plastic, which has led to the Kolkata Municipal Corporation ...

Egg Quality and Safety - Vikaspedia https://vikaspedia.in › health › beware-of-adulteration Plastic eggs or artificial eggs are a myth mainly due to the fact that there is no technology available to produce a plastic /

artificial egg that would ..."""

In order to understand the truth, just read the last link that I haveput in bold and underlined.

" Have we as humans, in any part of the world ever made a technological breakthrough to synthetically manufacture such true to type eggs?

Has science developed so much to put life into an egg?

Have humans become gods and found out the truth behind life, how life is made, perpetuated and stopped? Otherwise, how can you make an egg that does not rot, has the egg yolk and egg white sealed inside a shell in the perfect manner and still not leaking? Anybody with a little bit of sense in their heads would have easily thrown these arguments to the dustbin. But just imagine that all these media and many others flashed this rubbish in their columns and visuals?

What has happened to scientific temper and knowledge for the pressmen??

I bow my head in shame.

There are also videos in the You tube showing how fake cabbage is made. They say the Chinese do it. But even if it were true, how can you sell this painstakingly made cabbage at market prices? Funny that apart from making some leaves of cabbage, nobody has ever shown the manufacture of a fully round, perfectly bonded cabbage like the one that nature produces in the farmers' fields.

There are also many videos depicting the production, or finished product naming it as plastic rice? Are we so much foolish to believe that you can cook plastic rice with the smell of natural rice? Still further, is plastic and plastic rice making machinery so cheap to sell it in the market? If you scan ou tube, face book and Google, you can see thousands of foolish things that you would laugh at yourself.

And so, we have our brethren greatest fools in many other parts of the country, and deplorable still, in the media also.

Save the world, oh almighty.

Fools of the world unite,

for you have nothing to lose other than your brain

CHAPTER XX

Dhana akarshana yanthram and Nagamanikyam

This is about another cheating called as *Dhana akarshana yantram* or some other device like *Nagamanikyam* that supposedly, when kept in your house, will bring you lots of money again and again.

Have you ever heard of a device or material, which will continuously bring money to the person owning it or the house where it is kept? You might have heard in fables like that of Aladdin or Indian epic stories, where there can be a magic pot or bhooth(ghost) that will bring whatever it is asked for. It could be food of the choicest variety, very expensive and attractive clothes or, cash and gold coins. It should be admitted that every person of any religious faith or anybody from anywhere in the world would have heard such stories right from childhood. Without really knowing whether it is authentic or otherwise, we would also have told all these stories to our children or others. Of course, none of us have ever seen any such device working, and are the least sure of the existence of anything distantly similar to such a thing. But, since we ourselves have heard such stories umpteen number of times, and also have retold these stories to our kith and kin, as human beings, we still expect wonders to happen.

Almost all of us have this belief instilled in some corner of our subconscious or even conscious mind that there can be such a wonderful money making instrument somewhere hidden in this universe. So when some person approaches you that he has knowledge of such a thing, then many of us are destined to believe him. This conman or woman would call this as *Dhana Aakarshana yanthram* or any other similar name. Most of us also know that the meaning of this is "money attracting device". Humanity has never been able to unfold the truth behind life, and science, with all its wonderful developments, has not yet been able to create even a single celled organism and give life to it. So, there are still thousands of things that are unsolved, and we are tempted to believe in miracles or supposedly superstitious things. Things being so, if somebody claims that they have some object like a bronze statue or a securely covered pot with some magical thing inside or any other obscure object, people are bent to believe that they can bring money or wealth to the family.

"The argument that will run in the mind is that, may be this is not true, but I don't lose everything in my life. I am giving only some money to these people. So, if by sheer luck, this material brings in luck, let me have it.

This is where you are fooling yourself. There is also another very intelligent trick in this whole deal. You are made to understand that this is a very secretive and divine deal. If the truth behind the *Dhana aakarshana yanthram* is revealed to somebody, then, the power of the yanthram to bring in fortune and wealth will be lost. So, everything should be secretive. You should not tell anything about this even to your life partner or parents or other relatives or friends. It is also advised that these secret devises should always be concealed and nobody should be allowed to see it. These precautions from the side of the conman ensures that even when you are fooled to the core, you cannot complain to anybody, because there is absolutely no evidence of any transaction that took place between the conman and the conned. That is the real beauty of it.

There is yet another daylight, transparent, well-advertised fooling in another manner, using this very same trick. This is when some people advertise about the existence of this yantram, and even advertise the rates, mode of payment like prepaid or VPP etc. You also have the option to buy the ordinary, special, premium or extra strong yantram. The price of course is dependent on the strength of the yantram to bring money. Normally, they do send you the yantram also. This, in most instances, is something like a thin bronze plate with some geometrical design and Sanskrit shlokas (verses). Sometimes it is some other language (may be even gibberish) inscribed in the sheet. This can be framed like a wall hanging, and can be hung in a prominent place in the house or office etc. In this case, of course, there is no need to hide it. The rates are standard and when compared to the huge amounts of money involved in other methods of fooling, this is cheap going. Of course, when you buy it and place it in your house, whatever benefits that accrue to you are attributed to this, and when something bad happens, you blame it on destiny. Neither the seller nor the buyer feels anything sore about the deal, and they live happily ever on!!!!

Dhana aakarshan yanthram sample from the internet

Now about nagamanikyam. This is historically the "precious stone" that is formed inside the head of a cobra. This has been another favorite of fraudsters for long. The story of the precious stone being carried by the cobra or the King cobra etc. and the magical powers it has, in extracting the venom from the wound of a snake bite, and stories about the wealth it can bring to the person in possession of it, are all more than 2000 years old, and is popular in almost all countries of the world. Ruby or manikyam is a precious gemstone coloured deep pink or blood red. It has been mentioned in Vedic astrology to have the power to bring success in business, social status and wealth. Traditional snake bite curing doctors place such a stone above the snake bite area, and it absorbs the venom by capillary action. This is then put in milk to allow the venom to dissipate into the milk and thus make the stone ready for reuse. Mythology says that this ruby has its origin in Pathalam or the lower world (In Hindu Mythology, the Hell is supposedly below the earth, and the Heaven is up above us) and is the stone held by the snake king. The ones found in earth are very ferociously guarded by the king cobra and the like. It is believed that the unspent venom accumulating in the poison fang of the cobra gets solidified over the years into the ruby and is carried in the mouth of the snake. Some stories depict this as being carried as a throne above the head by the snake. In any case, the snake ruby is very precious and divine. During amavasi and pournami (new moon and full moon) the cobra will keep the ruby down and start praying with closed eyes. During these times, the tribal people will steal the ruby and keep it covered in cow dung. The snake, when it finishes the prayer, would look around to swallow the stone back, and when it can't find it, will hit its head in the rocks and commit suicide. The stone thief will then leave the place, wash the ruby in rose water and milk, and will keep it. This is the ruby that the fraudster describes that he bought paying a fortune and offering to willing customers. The legendary stone will supposedly radiate red hues at night.

People who fall for these descriptions end up paying anywhere between Rs.10 to 50 crores for the stone. The dealers camp in luxury hotels to lure in greedy customers looking to make a quick buck. There are various exaggerations that these fraudsters unleash to make the gullible fool to invest crores of rupees for an artificial stone that is not worth even a few hundred rupees. They will tell you stories that a successful hero of the movie world was a penniless commoner years back, and was languishing in the streets etc..He then purchased this ruby from this very same person years back and how he rose to the celebrity that he is now. It could otherwise be that of another business magnate being another client. Such make believe stories are told in many occasions to fool the poor fellows. It is made out that almost all billionaires in the world owe their riches to Nagamanikyam. Some of the five star or big hotels also are heard to be offering their clients to at least see such wonderful stone for a very meagre fee between Rs. 5000 to 25000. And many guests simply pay for this artificial gem fitted with a colour emitting LED below, and enclosed in a glass case. Over and above the Vedic astrological reference, in Kerala, there is also another reference to Nagamanikyam. This is in the book called ***Aithihyamala*** or tale of folklores, written by Kottarathil Shankunni. In this, there is a reference about the sacred serpent disguised as a stranger to have given such a stone to Pambumekattu Namboothiri, the then head of the family. However, they are a family of Namboothirees who are priests of serpent temples and also traditional vaidyas who rescue people from snake bites. As yet, there is no scientific established evidence about the existence of such a rare ruby. If you still believe in the power of a ruby to bring in wealth and fame, it would be advisable to buy gems only from a certified dealer. Many of us Keralites paid hefty sums for this Nagamanikyam or money attracting yantram, and got conned.

The question is, if that be so, why is it that the fellow who is selling the manikyam is not keeping it with him and becoming richer and richer???

Why should these people, sitting on a hillock of fortune, be selling it for a few crores, when they can get crores and crores every day from those manikyams or yantrams.?

Let me just tell you why. Even though we are one of the most intelligent populations in the world, we are also the greatest fools on earth. So, we dont ask these questions to him, but happily become a fool, paying hefty sums for an artificail ruby and dream of becoming the richest person in the world.

That is why we proudly call ourselves as Kerala-Fools own country.

CHAPTER XXI

Ice plus salt in fish is toxic

This again is propaganda against the poor fishmonger. Many photos are shown saying that fish is being stuffed with Ice and salt, and that this is toxic to humans. The description is made in such away as though the addition of common salt to ice is done so clandestinely and hiding it from the consumer.It is described as though they are doing a heinous crime and that if you consume such fish, kept in amixture of Ice and salt, you will have all sorts of stomach disorders, food poisoning and what not.

Here also, you are becoming the number one fool. The real fact in putting Ice and salt together is reproduced below.

"Salt Lowers the Temperature of Ice Water. When you add salt to ice (which always has an outer film of water, so it's technically ice water), the temperature can drop from freezing or 0 °C to as low as -21 °C. ... Salt lowers the freezing point of water via freezing point depression". Actually the components in the common freezing mixture for making ice cream is nothing but Ice and salt. In Europe and other cold countries, they have a system of adding salt or to be more specific, spraying salt solution on the roads during winter. The reason is that this will cause the freezing point of water to be lowered. In other words, water that forms ice at zero degree Celsius or 32 degree Fahrenheit will start freezing only at 20 degree Fahrenheit or minus 6.6 degrees. With the right combination, it could, as mentioned earlier, be as low as minus 21 degrees Celsius. The ice formed on the roads make it slippery and will cause vehicles to slip and cause accidents. It is to prevent this that they put salt solution. So there is absolutely nothing wrong to put salt into ice to lower its temperature.

The gossip mongers must also know that salt is one of the best and most common preservatives used to dry fish. Still to make a fool of us (and of course, the person himself) by saying that ice and salt is something deadly?? Oh, my god, what fools are we, to believe this, get panic stricken, and to aid the health of our near and dear, share it without even thinking about the most common things that we have been following since time immemorial.

The funny thing is that he or she who shares this deadly information might be doing that after enjoying a good meal spiced with dry fish curry that was salted all along. Because we Keralites have more education, and can read and write English and the rubbish that is propagated in the social media than most of our fellow mates in other parts of the country, we are the prime culprits in spreading this type of misinformation. Even a seventh standard child is taught this piece of information in their science syllabus that adding salt will lower the freezing point of Ice. So, how can somebody forward such foolish information that it is toxic to mix salt and ice? You have to be a grade one fool to reject that fish. Of course, I have warned you that we Keralites are also good in finding out excuses for not following something that is not convenient for us. So we are only selective fools when it comes to certain things. This sort of double standards and quick wit is something that we have imbibed from very early times.

There is a story about the witty poet of yesteryears, Kalakkath Kunchan nambiar, who is the father of the folk dance form called as Ottan Thullal. It is told that in the midst of a royal meal that Nambiar was enjoying along with the Maharaja, the King wanted to test the men around him. So when the sweet Milk payasam (Porridge) was served, the King just tasted it and said that the payasam was bitter. Everybody except Nambiar agreed, and stopped drinking the payasam. Nambiar enjoyed his portion and still asked for more. When the king asked why he was eating the bitter payasam, his reply was "Your majesty, I like the bitter taste of Sugar in the Payasam". That was sarcasm and clever reply at its height. But what we Keralites do by propagating falsehoods and foolishness, but cunningly avoiding it in our personal life, is nothing but double standards.

In a way, we are not real fools at least in some cases.Right?

CHAPTER XXII

Aquaponics.

I had already told you that we are good at following examples from around the globe, especially developed countries and also the Gulf. Many of us from Kerala are settled in various countries around the globe, and there are many relatives remaining back here. They also chat with these overseas relatives frequently, so that all of them are familiar with things abroad. For this reason, we have many things imbibed from those countries. We have McDonalds, and our children are enjoying all those foreign foods, which were unheard of for the common man till a few decades back. Those were the foods known only to those who read English novels. Now even the villages have many bakeries selling things similar to the ones in those eateries. Add to this, food like Al fam, kubboos, and many things native to the Persian gulf countries are available even in remote villages of the state.

A similar trend is to imbibe things that are common in other parts of the world. One such fad imitating what is practiced in western countries is the production of greens by aquaponics. This is a " food production system that couples aquaculture with hydroponics whereby nutrient rich aquaculture water is fed to hydroponically grown plants, where nitrifying bacteria convert ammonia into nitrates. The size, complexity and types of foods grown in this can vary as much as in any other farming system". In simple terms, you must understand that it involves all the requirements and paraphernalia of both aqua and hydroponics. So you nccd rcscrvoirs for growing fish, devices to aerate the water, and all precautions to see that the fish does not get killed by diseases. Mind you, if you were doing fish alone, you can go for a bigger scale with the same investment and effort. Since your production is only fish, with more care and management, you can get better yield and better profits. In hydroponics also, you need containers to hold the aqueous nutrient solutions, and circulating systems with pipes and other paraphernalia, and you have to select your crops. This is where the catch comes. In Europe, what they do with aqua or hydroponics is to grow greens in protected environments. That they do only because they consume a lot of greens in their food. **In India, if you were to eat raw greens like lettuce and spinach in sandwiches and salads the way they do, you will be more easily described as a cow, rather than as a human.**

A system showing aquaponics

So, we don't use that sort of greens in that many quantities anywhere in Kerala. But in imitating their style, various people have tried this and publicised in You tube and the like describing it as a very lucrative and wonderful idea. They also profess it to get fresh, chemical free organic healing type of vegetables and fresh fish. But if you watch their videos, it shows more of pipes, plastic buckets, and trays than anything green. ***In between this network of plastics, you may spot a lanky tomato holding an isolated fruit the way a poor mother holds her malnutritioned child.*** You might also see a few amaranths plants or one or two ladies finger plants with a shy fruit poking its nose outside. Europeans do it out of necessity and their food habits. Also, in our tropics, with scorching heat, you don't get even one tenth of what they produce as yield. In our wonderful state where we cannot survive without our rice, sambar, puttu, tapioca and the umpteen number of dishes that we savour, my humble suggestion is to use your brain **at least sparingly** to find out the cost benefit factors before you jump into the bandwagon of fools and get ridiculed for the rest of your life as an intelligent affluent fool not knowing what to do with his money. But if you still go for this system, fascinated by these videos, you are going in for a very expensive system(Your cost would run into at least Rs. 5, 00,000.), and end up getting a sprout of spinach, two ladies finger, a little bit of amaranths and a few peas in a season.

I don't kow how much you can get if you make a video and put it in You tube, about your successful aquaponics garden.

Other wise, if you spent this much money for a new venture to produce fresh fish and vegetables, but still order these items from outside for everyday use, will you not be a fool of the first order??

Come, join the bandwagon of fools

CHAPTER XXIII

Sambar with asafoetida

This is another wonderful foolishness that all Keralites swallowed without ever raising a single finger against. It is about an advertisement with one of the most popular film actors about a particular brand of Sambar powder.

You should know that sambar is the famous south Indian dish, and a readymade powder is used in some fast cooking. In the widely televised ad, the actor proudly announces that this brand is using an "XYZ" asafoetida as one of the ingredients and hence, is most superior in taste. Those who have at least a basic knowledge about sambar powder would know that the quantity of asafoetida in sambar powder is less than, may be one percent, and if you use any brand, the difference in taste in the ultimate sambar made with it may not be significant at all. It is as foolish as saying that if you are using a special brand of cuff button in a readymade shirt, the whole quality of the shirt is changed drastically. If the fellow is pulling the sleeves up, the button is never seen even. Let us, for argument sake, still admit that the asafoetida decides the destiny of the Sambar. So what was so special about this "XYZ" asafoetida? I googled the brand they were advertising and found that there was no such brand available in Google. Was it that a fictitious brand was used to promote a product or it was such a secret component that even google didn't know about it? May be.

We are forced to believe that theory just as we believe that in action scenes in movies, these lead role characters' fight with a dozen or so opponents, and in spite of being hit by hundreds of sticks, boulders or any other weapon, bounces back like a spring robot, and minces them all into dead meat in an action sequence that lasts for anywhere upto 10 or 15 minutes.

However, not to make us fools anymore, that ad was withdrawn after a few months of use. Was it that the other players in the field who were making similar sambar powders questioned the validity of the claim or did they put a complaint against this ad in the respective forum?

Or, was it that some non-fool amidst us questioned the Advertisement?

May be, not all of us are fools.

CHAPTER XXIV

Coastal regulation zone or CRZ

The teacher read from Wikipedia

"The Uruk period of Mesopotamia dates from about 4000 to 3100 BCE and provides the earliest signs of the existence of states in the Near East. Located along the Tigris and Euphrates rivers in the Middle East, the name given to that civilization, Mesopotamia, means "between rivers".

The Nile valley in Egypt had been home to agricultural settlements as early as 5500 BCE, but the growth of Ancient Egypt as a civilization began around 3100 BCE.[1]

A third civilization grew up along the Indus River around 3300 BCE in parts of what is now India and Pakistan (see Bronze Age India).

The fourth great river civilization emerged around 1700 BCE along the Yellow River in China.[2][3]

Civilizations tended to grow up in river valleys for a number of reasons. The most obvious is access to a usually reliable source of water for agriculture and other needs. Plentiful water and the enrichment of the soil due to annual floods made it possible to grow excess crops beyond what was needed to sustain an agricultural village. This allowed for some members of the community to engage in non-agricultural activities such as the construction of buildings and cities (the root of the word "civilization"), metalworking, trade, and social organization.[4][5] Boats on the river provided an easy and efficient way to transport people and goods, allowing for the development of trade and facilitating central control of outlying areas.[6]""

The student then asked

"Teacher, does that mean that from thousands of years back, people had been occupying the river banks and proceeded with agriculture, built houses and also establishments for industrial and day to day requirements, Right??"

Yes, that is what we read right now.

Are there constructions on the banks of major rivers of the world?

Yes, obviously.

You would have seen pictures of Venice, where the small canals and major tributaries of the lagoon shows tourists enjoying the scenic settlements from the boats, canoes and luxury yachts sailing through the river.

Listen, I will read more about it from Wikipedia

"The floating city of Venice, one of the most extraordinary cities in the world was built on 118 islands in the middle of the Venetian Lagoon at the head of the Adriatic Sea in Northern Italy. For travellers who have visited Venice and for those who have yet to go, Venice remains a beautiful mystery. It seems impossible for such a grand city to be floating in a lagoon of water, reeds and marshland. This is a place you must see to believe. Oh, why would anyone want to live on a flat, muddy, waterlogged island in the middle of a lagoon?

Fear!

People fled their homes on the mainland when barbarian conquerors were ravaging Italy in the 5th century A.D. They used the marshy lagoon for protection and found refuge among the poor fishermen living there. As the invasions continued across Italy, more and more refugees joined the first settlers and the need to build a new city grew. The famous city of Venice was born on Friday March 25th 421 AD (At high noon), just the beginning of the long and rich history for Venice.

How was Venice built

The floating city?

How Venice was built is its most fascinating story. When the new settlers arrived on the islands around 402 A.D., they were faced with the need for more space and a stronger foundation to live on. They had to find ways to strengthen the islands, drain them, enlarge them and protect the fragile environment. So, they dug hundreds of canals and shored up the banks with wood pilings. They also used similar wood pilings as foundations for their buildings. The settlers pounded thousands of wooden piles into the mud, so close together that they were touching. Then, they cut off the tops and created solid platforms for the foundations of their homes. Because the wood was underwater, it didn't rot. It's hard to believe, **but there are many buildings in Venice today that are still standing on 1000-year-old piles of wood!** Today, some people say Venice should be called the sinking city rather than the floating city. But, Venice began sinking the moment it was built. From the beginning, the weight of the city pushed down on the dirt and mud that it was built on, squeezing out water and compacting the soil. This phenomenon, together with the natural movement of high tides (called *acqua alta*) cause periodic flooding in the city, creating a sinking sensation. Over the past 100 years, the city has sunk nine inches. Some experts warn that global warming will cause sea levels to rise and eventually cover the Adriatic coastline and the city of Venice by 2100. Just like the first permanent inhabitants of these islands, Venetians today are trying to find ways to help their city endure and prosper.

Famous Russian writer, Alexander Herzen said: "To build a city where it is impossible to build a city is madness in itself, but to build there one of the most elegant and grandest of cities is the madness of genius."

I will show you a picture of current day Venice now.

A scene from Venice

If anyone were to see the settlements and buildings and development on the banks of any famous river, I would ask them to see the list below

Rome Italy Tiber
New York USA Hudson
Lahore Pakistan Ravi
Karachi Pakistan Indus
Paris France Seine
London England Thames
Moscow Russia Moskva
Washington DC USA Potomac
Basra Iraq Shatt-al-Arab
Cologne Germany Rhine
Delhi India Yamuna....

The list will grow if you scan more countries

Teacher, can you show us more photos of riverside cities?

I will show you one more from India, but search the net to see still more .

Allahabad, at the Triveni sangamam

If we were to see the situation in India, we would be delighted to know that many of the major cities in the country had their origin and development on the banks of rivers like the Indus, Ganges, Brahmaputra, Ravi, Beas, Sutlej, Cauvery, Krishna, Bharthapuzha and the like. Allahabad is an example and it lies close to Triveni Sangam, the "three-river confluence" of the Ganges, Yamuna and Sarasvati rivers.[1] It plays a central role in Hindu scriptures. The city finds its earliest reference as one of the world's oldest known cities in Hindu mythological texts and has been venerated as the holy city of Prayaga in the ancient Vedas. Allahabad was also known as Kosambi in the late Vedic period, named by the Kuru rulers of Hastinapur, who developed it as their capital. Kosambi was one of the greatest cities in India from the late Vedic period until the end of the Maurya Empire, with occupation continuing until the Gupta Empire. Since then, the city has been a political, cultural and administrative centre of the Doab region. In the early 17th century, Allahabad was a provincial capital in the Mughal Empire under the reign of Jahangir.[16]

Readers would now ask me why I am bringing up all these into this write up.

The answer is simple. There is a rule enacted by the Government of India, which regulates the living on the banks of the rivers, backwaters and the seashores in this country. **That is called the Coastal Regulation Zone rules.**

Basically, this is intended to save the riversides, seashores and the related areas of almost all waterbodies from any developmental activities to keep the pristine nature of the rivers and to prevent the encroachment of these lands for construction, housing industry and any other developmental activity. The zones would all be preserved in as is where is condition, and ideally, they would also be developed into greener areas like shrub jungle, mangroves, nature park for wildlife, birds and what not.

For this purpose, the land around these waterbodies have been classified into different CRZ zones.

If you ask why, the explanation in the rule is "" *with a view to conserve and protect the unique environment of coastal stretches and marine areas, besides livelihood security to the fisher communities and other local communities in the coastal areas and to promote sustainable development based on scientific principles taking into account the dangers of natural hazards, sea level rise due to global warming"".*

But the original script says that the declaration pertains to "the coastal stretches of the country and the water area up to its territorial water limit, excluding the islands of Andaman and Nicobar and Lakshadweep and the marine areas surrounding these islands, as Coastal Regulation Zone".

I thought I will reproduce the classification below. But that would be cruel. Primarily due to two reasons. Just read half a page of the original notification reproduced below.

*MINISTRY OF ENVIRONMENT, FOREST AND CLIMATE CHANGE NOTIFICATION New Delhi, the 18th January, 2019 G.S.R. 37(E).—**Whereas by notification of the Government of India in the erstwhile Ministry of Environment and Forests number S.O.19 (E), dated the 6th January, 2011 (hereinafter referred to as the Coastal Regulation Zone Notification, 2011),*** *the Central Government declared certain coastal stretches as Coastal Regulation Zone (hereinafter referred to as the CRZ) under section 3 of Environment (Protection) Act, 1986 (29 Of 1986); And Whereas, the Ministry of Environment, Forest and Climate Change has received representations from various coastal States and Union territories, besides other stakeholders, regarding certain provisions in the Coastal Regulation Zone Notification, 2011 related to management and conservation of marine and coastal ecosystems, development in coastal areas, eco-tourism, livelihood options and sustainable development of coastal communities etc.; And Whereas, various State Governments and Union territory administrations and stakeholders have requested the Ministry of Environment, Forest and Climate Change to address the concerns related to coastal environment and sustainable development with respect to the Coastal Regulation Zone Notification, 2011; And Whereas, the Ministry of Environment, Forest and Climate Change had constituted a Committee under the Chairmanship of Dr. Shailesh Nayak to examine various issues and concerns of coastal States and Union territories and various stakeholders, relating to the Coastal Regulation Zone Notification 2011 and to recommend appropriate changes in the said Notification; And Whereas, the report submitted by Dr. Shailesh Nayak Committee has been examined in the Ministry and consultations have been held with various stakeholders in this regard; And Whereas, a draft Coastal Regulation Zone Notification, 2018 was issued and hosted in the website of the Ministry of Environment, Forest and Climate Change on the 18th April, 2018 seeking comments and suggestions from all concerned; And Whereas, objections and suggestions received in response to the above mentioned draft Coastal Regulation Zone Notification, 2018 have been duly considered by the Central Government;*

First, did you understand anything?

Nothing,is it?

Neither did I get anything clear.

It is only utter confusion, right?

Secondly, the actual notification runs to 27 pages, and if your situation after reading just the first page is as though you have been struck at the back of your head, what would happen if you see the next 26 pages?. So I have decided not to eproduce it here.

So, when the officers who have to implement the decisions and the public are forced to read it, what remains is utter confusion. The officers, on their part to be on the safer side, would deny the benefits to the people who apply for construction, housing and the like, and the public would argue continuously for getting the things done. Obviously this is the fertile situation where bribing will flourish and also justice will be denied endlessly causing misery to the public. There are two things that you have to understand before you proceed further.

1. That this does not apply to Lakshadweep and Andaman Islands. The reason is also understandable because, if you are excluding 200 metres from the coast line in all the islands, and you draw the line from both the shores on tiny islands, one line might fall inside the other, and you may have to leave those islands fully free without even shifting a spadeful of sand forever.

2.Even though the preamble says it pertains to coastal zones, the description that comes further includes the riversides, backwaters and almost every side of every water body. For this purpose, and for creating confusion over compounded confusion, the declaration is almost a single line declaration, that runs to about 27 pages and crowned with comas, semicolons, numbering and all sorts of adorations.

Now let us consider the state of Kerala in the light of the above CRZ rules. Before we go into the details, we should understand that **"There are 44 major rivers in Kerala, a**ll but three originating in the Western Ghats. 41 of them flow westward and 3 eastwards. The rivers of Kerala are small, in terms of length, breadth and water discharge. The rivers flow faster, owing to the hilly terrain and also because of the short distance the rivers flow between the Western Ghats and the sea. All the rivers are entirely monsoon-fed and many of them shrink into rivulets or dry up completely during summer".

There are also 15 major backwaters in Kerala

More importantly, the coastline stretches to around 580 kilometres.

If we are to simply adopt all the rules as stipulated by CRZ, without ever raising any objections, there would be no space left for us to build anything, and if we were to stictly implement these rules, we may have to leave the state and find out home in any other state. These rules will not work in a land of rivers, their branches, backwaters and with one full side situated on the coastline.

But there is another side to this. Even after thes promulgation of these rules, the wealthy and influential are not affected at all. They build and propagate any where they want. So then,except these wise guys, the rest of us all , are we not the greatest fools on earth?

And to those high officials who stick on to and argue for the implementation of these rules. Over and above being most unethical, you are also forced to pretend to be blind in implementing these rules when it comes to influential people.

So, both the officials and the common public, are you not also the greatest fools on earth?

This outcry from my side, I should confess, is partly due to my own experience with the revenue officials and officials of the municipality.

I have my own experience that has been running for the past six years or so, and with the solution not anywhere in sight. You can add me to the list of greatest fools on earth, because I am a law abiding citizen. In 2015, I purchased 29 cents of land on the riverside, just adjacent to two or three self-occupied homes. I had dreamed of building a small place where I can spend some days in a year by the riverside, enjoying the calm and quiet village in the serene atmosphere with the cool breeze caressing me all the time. This plot had about 25 coconut palms in the whole of the land and the majority of them were more than 80 years old. Then in successive years, Kerala witnessed floods and landslides etc. As in any catastrophy, the poor were the most affected and were displaced from their homes. Of course you cannot call their dwelling places as homes as per the real standards, but to those poorest among the poor, those hutments were more than a palace. So I perceived some newer ideas in mind, and I thought of converting old shipping containers into safe and cheap dwelling homes for the poor. This theory I had to prove to myself, like cost factor, durability, air circulation, heat inside during day and cold during night and such other advantages and disadvantages. So, I bought a shipping container of 24x8 ft. dimension, made it into two rooms, with entrance on both sides, and a separation in the middle. People in this small place were seeing such a container in close quarters for the first time in their life and were naturally amused when the truck arrived.

Unloading container home

They were still amused when, (again for the first time in their life) they saw the whole container being lifted and unloaded to a set platform of solid steel T sections by using a Crain. Then, I converted this container into two separate bedrooms with false ceiling, side insulation, bulbs, fans, cupboard, mirror etc. just as in a double room in a standard hotel. Then I added two separate bathrooms also for the rooms. The whole set up just showed up as a temporary transportable arrangement, and had all the requirements for a tourist attraction. People could come there, enjoy the breeze, go to the riverside, take a swim, and also go fishing and enjoy the night by a campfire using just the coconut fronds that were freely available around. I am attaching here the photos of this nice ambience below.

caravan outside view

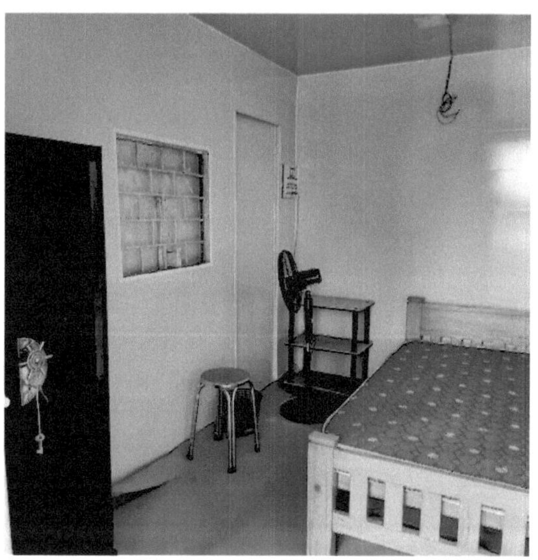

Inside view

The first obstacle to the project came when I wanted to put a little bit of soil around the hutment, to beautify the area and to get a small road access to the river. When the lorry came with a load of soil, the village officer personally came to the spot, threatened the driver and prevented the lorry load of soil from being unloaded. The load was sent back. I don't know if he has such policing powers but this is what happened. I was not present in the scene at that time, but came to know later, when and the lorry driver telephoned me and told this in the evening. The reason, as stated by the village officer, was that according to the village records, the land was nanja, which meant that it remained as wetland, just as in the case of lands where we do paddy cultivation. Interestingly, it is only in Malabar that this classification as nanja is given. It is misleading to the commoner because since the land is garden land with very old coconuts and with buildings all around, we never even dream that this can be classified as wetland. It is high time that such misleading words are replaced with common words in use that the ordinary citizen can understand. Coming back to the village officer, his overstepping of authority and taking the law into his own hands naturally irked me. But maybe he thought that I will approach him for a settlement offering something in return. **It is astonishing that a government official, who, normally may not even be available in his office during office hours for doing duty, sensed this lorry load being unloaded in his jurisdiction of at least a few squae kilometres with his sixth sense and overstepped his powers.**

By this time, I had spent a lot of money on the container caravan, and made it fully functional with two attached bedrooms and a first floor hall that can seat around 20 people or allow about 10 people as a dormitory, for school groups or the like. This would have been the perfect setting for an enchanting riverside holiday, enjoying a swim in the river and enjoying the cool breeze. They also have some youngsters with small canoes, who can take you to the water during night and do fishing live, with the tourists on board. The panoramic situation is still there, but I have to get permission for the caravan from the municipality. The first step for this is to get the land reclassified as garden land. So, I decided to go the way the law prescribed, and gave an application in 2019 for getting the land to be reclassified as garden land, observing all the procedures of filling up the application, adding additional supporting documents and the like. The official machinery went at its own pace, and in November 2020, I got a reply that the application for reclassification cannot be allowed. Interestingly, the letter, signed by none other than the Revenue Divisional officer had also stated that the land should be included in the databank and had instructed the village officer to prevent any construction in the land. **It also had an instruction to the Agricultural officer to take steps to include this land and every other land coming in this survey number in the data bank.** In other words, the instruction is to make this land as a paddy field, even though the lands in this survey number has dwelling places as old as 40 years, and also yielding coconuts not less than 80 years old. Obviously, the inclusion in the data bank is not in the purview of the RDO, and should be dealt with by an entirely different committee called as the local level monitoring committee which is not subservient to the RDO. There are various judgements in this regard, which clearly states that the Kerala Conservation of Paddy land and Wetland act 2008 should not affect the position of lands that are really garden lands and the ground situation of the land is the prime criterion which should decide the classification of the land. There cannot be any retrospective implementation of an order promulgated in 2008 to detrimentally affect the status of any land. But what am I supposed to do when something to the level of ignorance is perpetrated by a responsible government official? The order was based on a report of the very same village officer to had prevented the two loads of soil into my land. He had stated that the land is not in data bank, but he **understands** that there is a chance of flooding in the land. Mind you, it is only his understanding, and neither the superintendent or the RDO ever asked for any documentary evidence to prove that the land is prone to flooding. If this be the yardstick, then, half of Kerala will have to be declared as data bank. He also simply stated that the CRZ rules may have to be looked into.The CRZ rule is only for 50 metres from the High Tide , and also, there is an exception for tourist shacks and resorts. Even then, based on a gut feeling expressed by this village officer, with no documents backing up his intuitions, the RDO denied me justice, but also made atrocious decisions against me and everybody in the same survey number.

when I narrted this to friend, he told me a very wise solution that I should have done.

Imagine a situation like this.

I do not apply for a conversion or any building permit or so and continue with the occupation of the building, and even renting it out.Naturally, with the geneticlly orogrammed envy and crab syndrome instilled in our blood, one of the neighbours or any other well wisher would inform the autorities about the unauthorised construction. Naturally, they will rush to my place, and inspect. They will then issue ne anotice that my act is nt according to the law. I should follow the rules. They will atach all the application and other annexures required, and copies of documents reuired, and ask me to pay the fees, even including the payment challan. Because I am adefaulter, they would also impose afine on me. I can happily pay that without any other botheration and live happily ever after. They have the satisfation of penalising adefauler.

But I am happy too. Think of the situation if I were to apply in the regular manner. They will send me back at least ten times, asking for this revision, that revisionetc the way they have been doing to me for afew yeas. I have to waste may time and energy foall this. add to this, m inconveniences, and may be eveen the bribe that I would have had to ggive. But here, they have come to my place, and I am the King. They served my interests and I pay for it. Great going Right?

Now, let me again ask you whether we are not the greatest fools on earth, when,.................

When, we the most intelligent Keralite, with 44 rivers, 15 backwaters and a coastline of around 580 km, adopt the same CRZ rules as in the rest of India?

And, add to these geographical limitations, the hard reality that in some places, the width of Kerala is as low as 30 kilometres and the greatest width to the border is just 120 kilometres.

When you calculate the ratio of rivers, coastline, and backwaters to the actual geographical extent, we are just a miniscule area, fully filled with waterbodies, while other states are big brothers with just a few rivers.

And we both have the same rules. What a pity?

And our pig-headedness is doubled when you understand that these rules are applicable to the common man only and for the influential, it takes hardly a few minutes to get the approval done. Files are created with backdates, complete with objections, explanations, file noting's with different handwritings with different pens, accepting the explanation and overruling the silly objections, citing previous government orders, court rulings and what not. There are no uprisings or even a bold public outcry against this descrepancy, but what comes out is just fake claims about conservation of environment, carbon balancing, seaside protection, keeping the pristine waters clean and crystal clear and all sorts of cacophony. The powers that rule us are least bothered, since, these rules are not applicable to them.

Welcome to fools' own country

CHAPTER XXV

The covid Pandemic and wonderful way we fought it

There is a very famous book by O. Henry (This is the pen name. The real author is William Sydney Porter).

I will just tell you the crux of the story.

The stage is set during a pandemic of pneumonia in a village in England. It tells the story of an old artist who saves the life of a young girl suffering from pneumonia. Through her window she can see an old ivy creeper growing on a nearby wall and in the approach of winter, gradually shedding its leaves. She believes that when the last leaf falls, she will also die. The leaves fall day by day, but the last lone leaf stays on for several days. Every day seeing the leaf intact, she eventually gathers mental strength and comes back to life. Later we realise that this was done by an old artist by painting a classic work of the leaf on the wall the night before the last leaf fell. He did this, fighting the scorching cold for the whole night. However, the old man dies due to pneumonia that he contracts during the cold hours, but the young girl recovers. The story actually is to give a wonderful insight into human behavior and the ability of mental strength to fight all odds in providing the healing of ailments. It also underlines the ability of the human mind in giving the immune building capability that faith will instill in the human body. This probably is one of the reasons when you believe in god and start praying with the strongest resolve in your mind about gods' power to heal. Unbelievable miracles happen, during faith healings, mainly because the mind powers the body to build up resistance.

Science says that the body's resistance power is one of the best healing factors.

When you lose the confidence, you succumb to the foreign invading factor. If that be the case, what was the basis of the fear psychosis that was created in the minds of the whole populace by fomenting fears about the covid virus attack?

Was it not more appropriate to create a mindset for all of us by explaining the real threats, and the necessity for precautionary steps, and to say at least,

Let us face it boldly.

Be safe by taking all preventive measures.

Don't panic.

The government and the service minded people, the doctors and the whole health system is behind you.

Even in the unfortunate situation of anybody getting infected, even after the taking all the precautions don't panic. Be bold. Take all medicines, keep isolated for just a few days, and follow quarantine later. This is not the end of all.

In addition, to prove the point and to improve the general preparedness of the populace, it would have also been better to make videos of the survivors and to tell the public, that I have recovered; you too can pass the situation very lightly.

This should have been done at the very first instance, when the vaccine was not developed. After the vaccine, things could have been made more authentic, and reassuring.

I lament, at this point, that everybody, including the press, the visual media and the social media only created a panic about the pandemic.

To prove this point, let us now analyse the present situation when most of the population have been vaccinated twice and even the additional precautionary dose. The mindset in many of the persons that I met is no longer fear about the fever. Many even are prepared to face it if they get the fever. They feel that after the vaccination is complete, if the fever comes, it would just be a mild attack with not many severe symptoms. So, after that they will get some more immunity. And can be without the fear of getting the fever at least for the next three months. This is the sort of confidence that we had to develop even in the beginning situation. But what did we do?

Number one-

In the very first stage, we asked the people to remain indoors. The whole state was put under lockdown. The situation was not serious. It was premature to make a mountain out of a molehill. The number of cases were less than hundred or somewhere around that. It was that time when it was ripe to create awareness videos on the need to be cautious, and not to panic. It should have been more of a voluntary adoption of all precautions and loving persuasion to faithfully follow it. The reverse was done, and in a way, a sort of foolish implementation of the lockdown with an iron hand was done. The typical Keralite has a penchant to oppose prohibited things when he is not convinced. Even the very genuine things are usually opposed by a small fraction of people. Many are also inquisitive of who is doing what, against the rules and to watch those things surreptitiously. So, People especially youngsters, started to peep into roads, by lanes and streets, just to see who were all loitering. Obviously, they were not wearing masks, and were not aware of the seriousness of the impending doom. Many of the "do-nothing" people also continued to play rummy and the like in isolated grounds; they also played football and other games. Again, awareness creation was not there, but only a suppression of public living with an iron hand. Because the public never knew the seriousness of the symptoms, they failed in observing the protocols. We heard of police chasing these people, some falling into ditches, or abandoned wells and getting injured, some diving into rivers and getting lost and a lot of such mishaps. Was this the prudent way of fighting a pandemic?

Number two :

Did the full lockdown of the state for weeks and months do any good? Two years later, everybody accepts that it didn't. What it did was to put a stop to all life. Buses went off the road. There were only very limited shops. Except for the shops selling vegetables and groceries, every shop was closed. And, initially, there was a wonderful decision that vegetable shops would open on some days and groceries on some other day. So if you want to buy both, you have to loiter for two days. Wonderful brains, sir.

Obviously, the bus owners, shop owners, and the whole lot of people associated with all day to day activities became jobless paupers. People could not eat good food, hotels were closed, and it was those pathetic days. And to add to this, even when the lockdown was lifted, in parts of the state, in discontinuous bouts, the district collectors closed down their districts, special magistrates roamed around finding out violation of timings by shop keepers and to book the poor shopkeepers as though they were doing something unpardonable. To describe it otherwise it was as though your fundamental rights to pursue any profession were suspended. So, it was something like police raj in an undeclared emergency. Nobody questioned the scientific basis or even common sense behind this. Let me ask one thing. If all shops are closed for most of the time, when they are opened for a day in a week, or few hours in a day, will everybody crowd together to buy the items? And get infected?

Was it not more prudent to allow all shops to open at all times, so that the number of people visiting at any point of time will be so much reduced, and there will be very little personal contact? **'Wonder fool!!!**

I had certain doubts, about the virus, but I swallowed them wisely so as not to be branded as a fool by my learned bosses in the masses. The first thing that any virologist teaches you is that viruses need a living medium to survive. So, it might live in the saliva until it is dried, and that is the reason why you wear a mask to prevent the drop from entering your nostril or mouth. Okay, Agreed. But then, what is the need for putting two masks one over the other, when the first one itself is three layered? It only prevents normal breathing and eventually if you are using it continuously for hours together, you are definite to get breathing problems. In our state, all these decisions were taken by a committee headed by an MBBS doctor and many officials from the administrationas members. There were no virologists, pathologists, or experts from community medicine. Now, realizations have come very late. Persons who had the courage to point out these were never heard, but instead, were ridiculed and silenced. In Kerala, it is always the fool who frames and implement the rules and wise men keep mum. There is an adage in Malayalam that says, ***"maunam vidwanu bhooshanam***" which means, it is better for learned people to keep mum when fools start talking. I have to remind you that in the initial stages, the panic creation was so intense that even the driver of an ambulance who carried a covid patient was attacked by unruly mobs solely because he stepped out of the van. How miserable. The ambulance carrying covid patients were numbered 104, and just like in the the 1900s when people ran away from small pox victims, and dumped them in isolated places, the very sight of 104 Ambulance made people to flee. Why was this fear psychosis created and fostered by everybody who was at the helm of affairs, and the media?

Another funny thing that occurs even now and during the latter part of the pandemic, was that schools were closed, but the teachers had to come, even when there was no public conveyance. Also, even today when the vaccine has not been administered to the children below 12 years, what is the logic behind allowing them to school? Some reports say that prevalence of covid is low in kids. Still, even if one kid gets infected and succumbs to the fever, who will undo the loss of life? I don't see science or logic to support this decision.

During the lockdown and the restrictive phases, the police and sectoral magistrates were instructed to see that the closure of shops after the deadline was to be strictly followed and defaulters fined. Let me ask if I were in a shop at say 6 PM, after being in queue for essentials in many shops, and this shopkeeper has a few customers in front of his shop, what good will be served if he is forced to down the shutters at the stroke of the stipulated hour? These people invariably have to come again the next day or other day when the shop opens. In what way does it help in isolation and social distancing? The next day when they come again, getting into buses or scooter or whatever, and again clamouring for purchase, how is it that social distancing is implemented or does it defeat the very purpose? I had also witnessed a very sad scene when a teenager was mercilessly beaten by a police man, when he was waiting for his father who was buying medicines from the shop. The father came running to prevent his son getting beaten and even then the attitude of the policeman was very rude. Such instances of chasing people, scolding commuters, and all sorts of atrocities against the people, to say the least, was most unwanted. In every force, there are criminal minds. During occasions like these, these worthless goons will surface, and the majority of the disciplined force will have to swallow this misbehavior and shut their eyes. I had also felt sorry for these men in uniform, who had to wear the masks all the time, and be in the road, in the scorching heat and during torrential rain, just to implement these draconian instructions piped down from above by the high officials during meetings in air-conditioned conference halls. I had been worrying about their safety also, because, they were all dropped in their duty places in police jeeps, sitting clamoured and also sweating profusely. They probably never realised that the man sitting just beside is also a potential volcano of covid if they are not sitting observing social distancing. Just like saliva, sweat is also a liquid media from the body that, theoretically, can be a reservoir of the virus, much more than inert substances like currency notes or other non-living materials. So when you sit closely and the sweat gets into the surface of your body directly, it is a much more intense carrier of the virus than when it is airborne. Your mask is to protect from the airborne virus, but you are directly exposed here? What a wonderful idea, boss!!!

I have also seen poor shopkeepers being fined Rs.1000 because they were forced to keep the shop open for a few more minutes due to pressure from the buyers. Was that not cruel? His profit for the whole day might be less than that. He cannot ask his customer to get lost, because if he does, he loses his customer for ever. And, in another rule, it was stipulated that customers have to stay outside the shop, and only three persons can stay in front of one shop? Why 3? Why not 4 or 5? How did we arrive at the magical figure of 3? Should every shop owner install an automatic excluder for the 4th person outside his shop, or should he engage one person throughout to push out every fourth person? Foolishness and thoughtlessness of the nth grade, I would say.

Now, even in the third phase, where the covid cases, (probably omicron) started rising alarmingly and reached more than 50000 per day, this kneejerk reaction continued. One day it was that you can have 150 people for gatherings of political parties, but if it was for marriages and funerals, it should be 50. Does it mean that corona is ashamed of attacking politicians? Again, every day the allowed numbers got reduced, and one night it was reduced to just 20 for marriages. If I am right, in every marriage, there would be a bride and groom, and their parents. So, the siblings of the four parents themselves may be more than 20. And, there would also be the brothers or sisters of the bride and groom, and their kids. To them, the government's order is "Get out of the place, or you will be booked for violation of rules". So, in a marriage that occurs only once in a lifetime, you have to keep off even the direct siblings of the father and mother. Lucky that the number was not reduced to five or six, so that even the mother or father of the bride or groom should be asked to keep off the function.

Oh my Kerala, I love your corona war.

In this, there is another interesting thing. The Guruvayur temple witnesses something upto 100 marriages on most days. It was ordered that only 10 people can attend each marriage. If just 10 people attend each marriage, the total crowd will still be 1000. So, were you not forced to dilute the rules? When any decision is made, it has to be done considering all aspects of the situation and not some reaction, with the high handed attitude that we have been witnessing all these days. In democracy, there is only one day when the people are the kings- that is only for the few hours on the day of polling. For the next 5 years, in India, you are the slaves of the politicians whom you have elected. India is, without doubt the world's largest democracy {demo(n)crazy?}. Would it be better if we had a chance to be ruled by Kings and Rajas? When foolish and stubborn decisions are made, there would be the likes of Birbal and Thenali Raman, who by their wits and worldly wisdom will make the King realise how foolish he was. But of course, even the King has to be wise and learned, without ego, to be the beloved and loved.

Another funny thing is the Sunday lockdown to prevent the spread of covid. The holy bible says that god sat for creation for six days and took rest on the seventh day. Are you forcing covid virus also to take rest once a week by not providing humans as food? Great idea, sir.

It is also a decision with great wisdom that cinema halls are allowed half their strength, which would run to 300 to 500, while if it were a marriage hall, the corona will attack the 51st person. So that is why you have to keep the strength below 50. However, shopping malls can have many people, while in the supermarkets entry is restricted. At some time, it was also stipulated that they should switch off the Air conditioner. Those days, they were all heat chambers because such places were not built with fans, exhaust fans or ventilators. The air was stale which allowed the corona virus if any to remain in the humid sultry environment for a long time. Solely due to this reason, it defeated the very purpose of shutting off the AC.

And so, life continues as destined by these great experts and their most prudent, intelligent and scientific decisions to cut the corona virus to size.

My great Kerala, we are happy to be in this fools own country.

CHAPTER XXVI

Facebook is hiring

In this concluding chapter, I am happy to share with you that in our march to become the record holder in the Guinness book of world records for being the world's most literate and intelligent fools, we are not alone in this planet. There are again classical examples of all the world being fooled by using the social media apps like Facebook, and twitter and international brands like Coca cola and the like.

In this case, some fraud advertise that Facebook is hiring or Coca cola is hiring or twitter is hiring etc with impunity and ask for a small amount like one dollar, or to be more authentic, 99.99 dollars etc for processing the application for the jobs. The respondents would also share their personal information with these fraudsters, so that they can also sell this information. Any way, they get fooled. The funniest and intriguing thing is that Facebook, twitter,Coca cola etc get to know about this much later, or sometimes, they don't know it at all. Because, in many instances, these companies almost never warn the public that it was fake. How could a set of fraudsters so openly use these platforms for fooling the world's internet population? God alone knows.

However, when compared to us in Kerala, with all the above anti development skills that we have perfected over decades and still devising newer methods to halt development, let me proudly proclaim that we would be the only ones in the world where the per capita fools are the highest in the world.

We are happy that we are not alone in this fools' own earth

CHAPTER XXVII

Tailpiece: "Monson archaeological and artefacts museum for the greatest accredited fools on earth"."

This latest incident is the crowning glory in Kerala fools' coveted throne. It is said that you can fool everybody for some time and somebody for all times, but you can't fool everybody for all times.

This is the story of five-star fooling of very intelligent fools for a considerably long time and can be described as the **"Monson archaeological and artefacts museum for the greatest accredited fools on earth".** All the information that is described in this part are excerpts from newspapers and other sources in public domain. This person, Monson Mavunkal was arrested by the state police in an action complete with cinema style drama. There is a cheating case, and many other cases against this person. Many other enforcement department cases and enquiries are also going on, and many of them are in court.

Let us just read about some of the very interesting acts of this person

Have you ever thought that you can get two silver coins from the 30 coins that were given as bribe to Judas to identify Jesus Christ? Must be more than 2000 years old, that is, older than the Christian era itself, right. Well, we have this Monson having two coins from among those 30 that Judas got. It is one of the most prized possessions in the multimillion dollar worth collection of this ***antique collector cum doctor cosmetologist cum businessman cum friend of the sheiks and rulers of the countries and kingdoms of the Persian Gulf, and what not.*** Any high school student will ask at least ten questions to prove the authenticity of this claim before believing this flattery. Yet, very many most intelligent and influential people from all walks of life in this "fools' own country" believed this as true. Not just that, they also proudly proclaimed in public that they were lucky enough to have seen all this with their own eyes and were blessed by the almighty to be one of the few who were so blessed.

Another of the other rarest and most divine collections was a piece of loincloth that was used to wipe the face of Jesus when he was brought down from the cross. People tend to believe that a piece of cloth that is more than

2000 years old does not have the looks of antiquity, but resembles a piece that would have been produced from a loom just about a few years back. To counter those doubting Thomas's, you are also made to believe that the strength of that divine piece of cloth is that even though it is more than 2000 years old, it still looks as though it was new. **(You are flattered")** Just think how powerful Jesus is. When you believe in something, especially connected to faith and religion, you don't suspect, right? That is the weak point where these fraudsters exploit and make you gullible.

If you are lucky enough and a VVIP powerful enough to be associated with this antique collector to enter the (fake) rarest of rare museums that this man has in his private collection, you can also be lucky to have a glance of the M**ud cross** that was made out of the soil from ***Gagultha***, the place that bore the footprints of Jesus on his way to crucifixion.

You can also be glorified to see with your own eyes, and may be even to touch the holy garland in the collection that was made from the threads of the hand towel that was used to wipe the face of Jesus Christ.

Biblical evidences proclaim that Jesus converted water into vine. In a wedding function, at Cana in Galilee, all the wine they had bought, was exhausted. Guests were still coming. Jesus saw that there were six stone jars nearby, the kind used by Jews for ceremonial washing, each holding from twenty to thirty gallons. Jesus asked the servants there to fill the jars to the brim. Then he asked them to draw some of that water and take it to the master of the banquet. The master of the banquet tasted it and proclaimed to the bridegroom that they have saved the finest vine till last."

Monson also has one of those six stone jars! How wonderful??? Again, you are blessed to have had a glance of that holy pot.

Monson had people believe that he was in possession of the holy remnants or artifacts belonging to 28 ordained saints.

The staff of Moses is mentioned in the bible and Quran as a walking stick used by Moses. It was used to produce water from a rock, was transformed into a snake and back, and was also used at the parting of the Red sea to lead the Israelites out of Egypt and from slavery. And who was Moses? He is considered the most important prophet of Judaism, and also of Christianity, Islam, Druze faith, Bahai faith and other Abrahamic religions. Moses is supposed to have lived at least 13 centuries BCE (or BC) So to date, the antiquity of Moses must date back to around 3300 years. So, if I have the staff of Moses in my collection, what else is needed to make my whole collection priceless? Monson had this Moses' staff in his collection!!!! And all the fools who visited his collection took pride in having at least seen the staff.

Moses with his staff

The above is a depiction of moses from the internet. He helped israelis to cross the Red sea.According to the Book of Exodus, the staff (Hebrew: מַטֶּה matteh, translated "rod" in the King James Bible) was used to produce water from a rock, was transformed into a snake and back, and was used at the parting of the Red Sea.In other depictions, the staff had a snake on it, and was to help the israelis to escape from snake bite . The snakes bit them when they questioned the lord and also Moses.

Now, Monson showed a staff that he claimed as Moses Staff. The handle part of this is shaped like a serpent and is just an ordinary fancy walking stick made by some artistic minded person a few decades back, according to the person who sold it to Monson. An antique dealer, Santhosh Elamakkara, who normally supplies materials for film shooting, has testified that he sold the particular walking stick, collected from some house in Thrissur, as a mere walking stick. And laments that he still has to get the payment for it.

Another of the holy artifacts in this rarest of rare fake collections is a piece of nail that belonged to St. Antony. I don't know whether it was St. Antony of Padua, (*Antonio di Padova-* Italian; also, *Antonio de Lisboa,* Anthony of Lisbon- Portuguese Lived between *1195 and 1231*) or Anthony the Great, Christian Monk of Egypt, *251-356AD.* St. Antony of Padua is invoked for return of lost property. The Egyptian saint is also known as father of all monks, and is appealed to get rid of infectious diseases. In either case, you are made to believe to be lucky enough to have a glimpse of a holy object. Mind you, in any case, the nail should be at least eight centuries old. Commonly, we see that if you cut your nail and throw it off, they will be lifted by ants immediately. Or, otherwise, it gets decayed naturally in a matter of a few months. But this nail, to have survived this many centuries, ho ho ho! How holy and revered.

Praise the lord, praise the lord, halleeluyya, halleluyya.

In Kerala, many believers pray to St. Alphonsa of Bharananganam for cure of diseases and many other blessings in life. She was beatified in 1986 and canonized in 2008 by the Vatican. Again, Monson made people to believe that he was in possession of a Piece of St. Alphonsa's veil. To make a rag cloth to be faked as this holy object, it is not just courage or even Dutch courage, but unscrupulousness of the nth kind, to make a mockery of sacred faith and belief.

Kuriakose Elias Chavara was a Syro – Malabar Catholic Priest, Philosopher and social reformer. He is considered the first canonized catholic male saint of Indian origin. Beatified in 1986 and canonized by Pope Francis at Rome in 2014. He is fondly and reverently referred to as Chavara Achan and is believed to bring in miracles in the lives of the believers. There are a lot of people who pray to Chavara Achan. Monson did not spare Chavara Achan even and showed dresses and gown that he claimed to have belonged to this ordained holy soul. And a lot of people stood spell bound viewing the depth of the religious collection of ancient artefacts that Monson had in his private museum. To add to all these holy collection, he also had a copy of the bible written in real gold pages. How wonderful, costly and revered? People would no doubt be thunderstruck and will instantly be mesmerized to bow in reverence to all these holy things.

Another of the priceless collection is the original new testament written by Matthew in his own handwriting.

He is also having Mother Theresa's Hair in his collection.

Many of these **wonderful original fakes** can be seen in his own website ***www.monsonmavunkal.com.*** He is introduced as a peace promoter, Philanthropist, educationist, speaker and motivator, cosmetologist, antique collector, actor and what not.

Now if you think that he was well versed only in Christian mythology, you are mistaken.

He has wonderful imagination, and a small wooden butter pot (Here there is a confusion. Many newsfeeds describe this as Uri. Actually, Uri is the hanging structure to keep pots with curd or ghee or butter (or in Kerala, even dry fish or dried meat inside). This structure is made of rope.

I don't know whether monsoon described it as Uri or butter pot, but what I remember to have seen in his hand is a small wooden pot the size of a cricket ball). There is also another photo that shows a dilapidated pot with some rope around it. I am not sure which one is **the original fake.** This was one among the many articles which was sold as a curio for the showcase and the person who sold it says he collected it from some house in Palakkad. But Monson developed a story for this small pot to have a link with Lord Krishna himself. Most of us know that Krishna, as a child was depicted to be addicted to freshly churned butter and has been called as Makhan Chor (butter thief). There are very many paintings and other depictions where the small kid Krishna is shown as climbing on wooden mortar and stealing butter from the pot in the Uri. In many instances, he catches the mud pot with the butter, and eventually falls along with the pot and butter. In the process, the pot breaks. Krishna would then start eating the butter that is splashed around. Now, Monson got a small Uri from this curios dealer Santhosh Elamakkara. His imagination ran wild and he concocted a very intelligent story about Lord Krishna. The story was that to prevent the nuisance of Krishna breaking the pot in his attempts to steal butter, Yashoda, Krishna's foster mother invented a solution. That was to make a wooden butter pot in the Uri, so that even if it falls to the ground, only the butter spills, but the butter pot does not break. That imaginary wooden butter pot from Krishna's time, (about 3000 to 5000 years old) is what he is now having in his collection. I would say that you must be having not just imagination or even courage, but should also be an extreme dumb head to makeup such a story. Those who believed it to be true and queued up to have a holy darshan of it, can we limit them to be called as Just fools? If the cricket ball sized pot is the original fake, then I doubt the intellectual sanity of those who believed that Yashoda made a pot that could hold just around an ounce of butter alone, in a society where the everyday collection of butter in those households must run to at least a few kilograms. Forgive me, Oh Lord, for disbelieving in your wonderful capabilities to hold a few kilograms of butter in an ice cream ball.

To attract people from Islam, and may be also to show that he liked all religions, there was an oil lamp, resembling the ones used by the Jews in Cochin and must have been around hundred years old. This was publicized as an earthen lamp used by Prophet Mohammed himself. Monson, in one of the videos, is seen explaining that this is a wonderful lamp, where you pour olive oil through a hole on the underside, and then tilt it to keep upright with the hole below, but not a drop of oil spills down. Then Mohammed, the prophet would light up the lamp. Wonderfully holy, right? So, people from the Muslim religion are also naturally attracted to Monson.

(There is nothing unusual about it. Any container with a hole below will not leak, unless there is a hole above also. Your sewing machine's oil bottle, even when you keep it upside down, will not leak, unless you press it. That's science, where you need the atmospheric pressure on both sides for the liquid to come out). But it is easy to fool believers, right? Monson claims that he has the largest collection of the Holy Quran collected from different parts of the world, and must be the largest outside the Arab world. (Monson, however is good at giving talks about religious harmony and tolerance, the worthlessness of hatred, how miniscule humans are in this universe, and a lot of other things. That is one charisma you should appreciate and applaud. Also, many from the general public is of the opinion that Monson gave some of his money for charity and aiding the poor. He has never cheated any poor man and has only duped very rich people). Now, that goes to his credit, and I appreciae his caring for the poor.

Ancient Siva Lingam, Buddha statue, centuries old Bhagavat Githa, Sri Sai baba's golden sandals, Paintings of Leonardo da Vinci, Picasso and Raja Ravi Varma, the ring of Aurangzeb's wife, The Original Nandi Statue, the first ever gramophone produced in the world are some other important items in his collection. The funny part is that in these days of information explosion, a simple search in the most ordinary cell phone can instantly reveal the truth about all these things. With that in your own hands and fingertips, it is just only in this fool's paradise that people of all genre (Film Actors and actresses, writers, Police top brass, Playwrights, and a veritable who's who in the country) queues up to accredit themselves as the world's greatest fools. What a pity .

Tippus throne.

Monson made photographs with former Kerala DGP Loknath Behra sitting on the a throne that supposedly belonged to Tippu sultan,the Mysore warrior of yesteryears, who fought against the british and was killed by them at Srirangapatanam. Just beside him was ADGP Manoj Abraham holding the sword of Tippu.

(Needless to say, both were fakes but unfortunately, fakes of very poor workmanship.We would feel pity for the chair that was depicted as the throne)

A very poor imitation of the great throne of Tipu Sultan

You can search the internet to see depictions of the original throne and how elaborate and costly it was. Tipu sat with his legs folded.

Information says that after the defeat of Tippu at Srirangapatnam, the army looted Tippu's palace and the royal gold plated throne was cut into pieces and taken to England. Some pieces were auctioned later. This information is available in the internet with the photo of the original from different angles, showing the peacock above and the tiger below. What Monson made by a carpenter from Chertala, a nearby town was a single seater with the tiger head resembling more as a sick lioness rather than a tiger. Probably Behra and Manoj Abraham got suspicious, and their enquiries with the Govt of India made the undoing of Monson.

Another wonderful item in his collection is said to be the World's first organ. Celebrated artists also got fooled by this man. One such case is that of a very gifted and famous keyboard player, renowned in the whole of south

Indian film and music industry. This celebrity musician was seen in a video praising Monson that he was lucky to see the world's first organ in this man's collection.

He should have at least verified this before proclaiming this in a public function and being branded as a gifted fool for the rest of his life. Information from Wikipedia about the world's first organ is reproduced below.

The earliest known organ was the hydraulis of the 3rd century BCE, a rudimentary Greek invention, with the wind regulated by water pressure. The first recorded appearance of an exclusively bellow-fed organ, however, was not until almost 400 years later. By the 8th century organs were being built in Europe, and from the 10th century their association with the church had been established. The 15th and 16th centuries witnessed significant tonal and mechanical advances and the emergence of national schools of organ building. By the early 17th century all the essential elements of the instrument had been developed, and subsequent developments involved either tonal changes or technological refinements.

The origins of the pipe organ can be traced back to the hydraulis in Ancient Greece, in the 3rd century BC,[5] in which the wind supply was created by the weight of displaced water in an airtight container. By the 6th or 7th century AD, bellows were used to supply Byzantine organs with wind.[5][6] A pipe organ with "great leaden pipes" was sent to the West by the Byzantine emperor Constantine V as a gift to Pepin the Short, King of the Franks, in 757.[7] Pepin's son Charlemagne requested a similar organ for his chapel in Aachen in 812, beginning the pipe organ's establishment in Western European church music.[8] In England, "The first organ of which any detailed record exists was built in Winchester Cathedral in the 10th century. It was a huge machine with 400 pipes, which needed two men to play it and 70 men to blow it, and its sound could be heard throughout the city."[9] Beginning in the 12th century, the organ began to evolve into a complex instrument capable of producing different timbres. By the 17th century, most of the sounds available on the modern classical organ had been developed.[10] From that time, the pipe organ was the most complex man-made device[11]—a distinction it retained until it was displaced by the telephone exchange in the late 19th century.[12]

The pipe organ in Saint-Germain l'Auxerrois, Paris

With this much information available in your fingertips in a mobile phone, people still make themselves the greatest fools on earth by believing scrap fakes as genuine, and still further, to publicly proclaim it to make themselves the greatest fools on earth. How do you describe that??

Another musical celebrity showed a ring in his fingers as being studded with a black diamond and proclaimed it as having been gifted by this very same person. Needless to say, it was an original fake!!!

The duping History

Monson was arrested based on a complaint by 10 businessmen that they were duped of around ten crores each, by offering handsome returns or priceless antiques. Monson's rented house showcased a large number of very costly cars of very famous brands, with carefully cultivated propaganda as to have belonged to celebrities like Amitabh Bachan, or some Bollywood actress or the like. To speak the truth, many were modified fakes, and were not roadworthy, but just museum fakes. In typical Monson style, the amounts due to the car supplier were also not fully paid, it is reported. No one dared to complain against Monson, because, he had carefully articulated close contacts with the top brass of the Kerala Police, Celebrities from the film Industry and also Political heavyweights. Photos of Monson with these VIPs were also prominently displayed in his rented house. When arrested, true to his character, the rent for the house for eight months was also pending. He had made people believe that an amount of Rs. 2.62,0000 lakh crores **(Dont faint when you really think of all that money)** were pending in a private bank in its Delhi branch and also showed them the receipts (Fake, of course) from the bank towards this. He made people believe that this was the amount paid to him by members of the Royal families in many gulf countries. He maintained that this amount was withheld because of the Foreign Exchange Management Act, FEMA, and will be released soon when the Govt of India verifies the legitimate documents that he had already produced to the ministry. He also made people believe that he was in the antique and diamond business for the past 25 years., "For close to a decade, 52-year-old monsoon Mavunkal used a mixture of deceit, charisma and carefully cultivated influence to make the implausible possible. He donned the roles of motivational speaker,doctor, cosmetologist, art promoter, antique collector, you tube star, and what not. He was arrested on the occasion of the engagement of his daughter, from his rented house in Cochin. The local police were not informed of the operation, and as soon as the engagement function was over, policemen in plainclothes in spite of stiff resistance from his security guards, took the con star into custody. Even this episode had its cup of comedy and fraud, since even the weapons that the guards wielded against the special crime branch force that undertook the operation, were mere toys!

Monson always used a small portion of the money that he duped, for small acts of charity, that was very cleverly publicized in all forms of media. He also made it sure to felicitate the top police chiefs of the state whenever there was a change of guard at the top levels. He made it particular to take photographs with them and to publicize in the media and to display them prominently in his museum of the rented house, so that others who happened to visit were unknowingly made to realise how influential this man was. It was also his habit to receive celebrities from cinema, social activists, and all people who were worthy of being photographed with. He intelligently used these photos to make people believe that he was in closeness to people like the Sultan of Brunei, Prime Minister Narendra Modi etc. He was also unscrupulous in cheating even the poor artists and craftsmen who made articles for him, by not paying them their worth of money for their work. These articles were then transformed as antiques, and were to be sold at fancy prices to rich people who were art collectors. It is also wonderful that this man, who does not even have a valid Indian passport, was reported to have travelled around the globe, at his own will and pleasure, indicating the excellent conning skills that he possessed. Interestingly, even though he has been charged of conning people to the extent of a minimum of 500 crores, his account has only around 50 lakhs and another 50 lakhs that are in the accounts of his employees. The funny thing is that the arrest of Monson was primarily based on complaints from six businessmen that they paid 10 crores each to this man (may be for fancied returns) and was duped by him. Where is all this conned wealth, then??Monson (God?) alone knows!!!!

The latest addition to his crime record is that he has also been charged under the Protection of Children from Sexual Offences (POCSO) Act on Tuesday, October 19. He was charged based on a complaint filed by the daughter of a staff member at Monson's cosmetic centre. In the complaint, it is alleged that Monson had sexually molested the then minor girl several times since 2019 and impregnated her, after offering to help her in getting admission for higher studies. The police said that the accused had abused the survivor many times at his rented house in Kaloor, Ernakulam. Their report is that the family of the survivor feared lodging a complaint as they assumed that Monson had close connections with influential people. It was after his arrest in a cheating case that the survivor and her family dared to file their complaint, police said. Police also suspect that Monson has been abusing other students from economically poor backgrounds, promising to help them in higher studies.

Monson Mavunkal, who established a museum in Kochi with fake antiques, was arrested on September 26,2021 by the Kerala Crime Branch for allegedly swindling money. Many influential people, including former Director General of Police Loknath Behera, Additional Director General of Police Manoj Abraham, political leaders, actors and many other celebrities, had visited his museum. The photos of them with Monson had circulated on social media soon after the arrest".

In a rare twist of events where the fraudster himself was conned, Monson has complained that he was duped of around 20 lakhs by one Anita Pulleyil, a Keralite lady with an Italian connection. Anita agrees that Monson had given the money that she spent for the wedding of her sister or so, but maintains that it was some fees that she was entitled to get. Peanuts, as it may be, but whom should we congratulate?

My humble suggestion is that this imaginative fraudster be made a part of the fake detection department in the police force to detect fakes and to detain criminals with this evidence. There is a story running along these lines. A boy in his teens made a wonderful hacking in the US by getting into the US treasury. He made a hacking where an amount of just 0.25 cents would be siphoned off into his personal account from every social security pensioner in the country every month. Needless to say, when pooled together, it made a fortune for the boy. But he got caught when a great old grandmother in her nineties, who had a habit of checking her pension meticulously every month, noticed that the decimal fraction of her pension was not the same that she was entitled and made a complaint. The department,made an investigation, and found out the hacker boy. However, they did not punish the boy, but absorbed him in the anti-hacking section to prevent such frauds from intelligent hackers. Why not we follow the great example and give him a job as an assessor of antiques? So come on fools, let us clap our hands in approval for this wonderful decision.

Fools of the world unite; you have nothing to lose other than your self-respect. (With apologies to Marx and Engels)

P.S. I had seen videos of many of the artefacts in the collection of Monson. Many of them, even though not antique pieces, are worth visiting. Many have very good appeal and even as simple artefacts, must be costly enough to make the whole collection worth at least a few crores. It should have taken at least some years of persistent effort to make such a collection. Had he not overstepped his imagination into duping, he could have well been a private collector of worthy artefacts.

Epilogue

The world over, there are fools. But our case in Kerala is unique for being very educated, but still wonderful fools. We will never learn. Even after another ten years, if anybody among us is observing, they can write another book of foolsih acts, even lengthier than the Mahabharatha.

If only we had the time to verify the obvious foolish things!!!

www.ingramcontent.com/pod-product-compliance
Ingram Content Group UK Ltd.
Pitfield, Milton Keynes, MK11 3LW, UK
UKHW041640190726
13854UKWH00006B/2614

9 798887 339382